THE
WORST-CASE SCENARIO
SURVIVAL HANDBOOK®

APOCALYPSE

THE
WORST-CASE SCENARIO
SURVIVAL HANDBOOK®

APOCALYPSE

By Joshua Piven and David Borgenicht
Illustrations by Mike Rogalski/Eyewash

QUIRK BOOKS
PHILADELPHIA

Library of Congress Cataloging in Publication Data
Names: Piven, Joshua, author. | Borgenicht, David, author.
Title: The worst-case scenario survival handbook. Apocalypse / by
    Joshua Piven and David Borgenicht ; illustrations by Mike Rogalski/
    Eyewash.
Other titles: Apocalypse
Description: Philadelphia : Quirk Books, 2023. | Summary: "A collection
    of survival advice from subject experts on a range of apocalyptic
    scenarios from practical to fantastic"– Provided by publisher.
Identifiers: LCCN 2023018319 (print) | LCCN 2023018320 (ebook) |
    ISBN 9781683693550 (hardcover) | ISBN 9781683693567 (ebook)
Subjects: LCSH: Survival–Handbooks, manuals, etc.
Classification: LCC GF86 .P5825 2023 (print) | LCC GF86 (ebook) |
    DDC 613.6/9–dc23/eng/20230505
LC record available at https://lccn.loc.gov/2023018319
LC ebook record available at https://lccn.loc.gov/2023018320

ISBN: 978-1-68369-355-0

Printed in China

Typeset in Adobe Caslon Pro, Arial, Avenir Next LT Pro, FFDingbats, and Whitney

Designed by Paige Graff
Interior illustrations by Mike Rogalski/Eyewash
Production management by John J. McGurk

Quirk Books
215 Church Street
Philadelphia, PA 19106
quirkbooks.com

10 9 8 7 6 5 4 3 2 1

WARNING

When a life is imperiled or a dire situation is at hand, safe alternatives may not exist. To deal with the worst-case scenarios presented in this book, we highly recommend—insist, actually—that the best course of action is to consult a professionally trained expert. DO NOT ATTEMPT TO UNDERTAKE ANY OF THE ACTIVITIES DESCRIBED IN THIS BOOK YOURSELF. But because highly trained professionals may not always be available when the safety of individuals is at risk, we have asked experts on various subjects to describe the techniques they might employ in those emergency situations. THE PUBLISHER, AUTHORS, AND EXPERTS DISCLAIM ANY LIABILITY from any injury that may result from the use, proper or improper, of the information contained in this book. All the information in this book comes directly from experts in the situation at hand, but we do not guarantee that the information contained herein is complete, safe, or accurate, nor should it be considered a substitute for your good judgment and common sense. And finally, nothing in this book should be construed or interpreted to infringe on the rights of other persons or to violate criminal statutes: we urge you to obey all laws and respect all rights, including property rights, of others—even after the apocalypse.

—The Authors

CONTENTS

11   **Foreword**

16   **Introduction**

PREPPING 101

20   How to Not Panic When You Think the World
      Is About to End

24   How to Pack a Go Bag in Thirty Minutes

28   How to Apocalypse-Proof Your Finances

34   How to Prep Your Bunker

40   How to Make Your Bunker Feel Like Home

44   How to Hide Your Preparedness

46   How to Hide Out in the Wilderness

50   How to Relocate to Another Country

APOCALYPTIC EVENTS

60   How to Survive an Alien Invasion

73   How to Outwit a Zombie Horde

78   How to Defeat a Global Supercomputer

82   How to Fight a Robot Uprising

88   How to Survive a Superflood

92   How to Survive Wildfires

99   How to Survive a Tsunami

102   How to Survive a Supervolcano Eruption

105   How to Survive an Asteroid Crash

111   How to Survive the Next Pandemic

115   How to Survive a Nuclear Disaster

122   How to Deal with Fallout

SURVIVING THE AFTERMATH

130   How to Determine If Conditions Are Safe

133   How to Make an Emergency Air Filter

136   How to Make an Emergency Gas Mask

143   How to Locate Other Opportunistic Tools (LOOT)

145   How to Make Hunting Tools

153   How to Skin Animals and Tan Hides

156   How to Eat Insects and Rodents

160   How to Forage

166   How to Determine Who to Eat First

168   How to Drink Your Own Urine

177   How to Build Shelter in an Extreme Climate

184   How to Sleep in a Bear Carcass

186   How to Plant a Survival Garden

191   How to Build a Composter

194   How to Locate Other Survivors

198   How to Communicate over Distance

DANGEROUS CREATURES AND HUMANS

208 How to Fend Off a Pack of Wolves

211 How to Fight Big Cats

213 How to Befriend a Gorilla

220 How to Escape Cloned Dinosaurs

225 How to Befriend Neanderthals

228 How to Fend Off Swarms

234 How to Fend Off Hostile Clans

238 How to Merge with Another Clan

242 How to Write a Constitution

245 How to Ethically Repopulate

248 How to Rebuild a Utopian Society

252 **Experts and Sources**

263 **About the Authors**

FOREWORD

Historically speaking, it is hard to dispute that the one thing all great civilizations have in common is that they will all eventually collapse.

With the climate and world politics in their current states of deterioration, we are at a point in human civilization where it would be prudent to sit up, take notice of what is going on, and prepare for the, well, uncomfortable events that could be coming our way sooner rather than later.

That's my area of expertise. I served in the British Army for twenty-one years as a Combat Engineer and Mountain Leader, traveling the world to hostile or otherwise challenging locations. When I left the military, I was hired as a civilian instructor for the Army in the Canadian Rockies, teaching mountain survival and traveling skills. For a short while, I also taught "critical infrastructure protection" with an NGO, where I used my military training to teach government groups how to protect key assets such as roads, pipelines, or main installations against theft or terrorist attack. And now I am a wilderness living skills and survival instructor, an herbalist, and a wilderness first aid instructor. I also consult for the world of TV. I have worked on many shows but lately my main role has been as Lead Survival

Consultant for the History Channel show *Alone*.

So I have a lifetime of training and stories behind me. When I teach groups about disaster readiness, the story I tell the most took place in the sleepy mountain town where I once lived in the Canadian Rockies.

It was June 2013 when the skies opened and a deluge of water fell from above, soaking the tops of the mountains and melting the snow. The result was a 100-year flood. Water smashed into our town and destroyed complete communities in our province. It was later recorded as one of Canada's most expensive natural disasters.

My family and I were directed to a local evacuation center. We all arrived fully dressed and equipped for a weeklong backpacking trip in the mountains. We also carried a bag of medical supplies and food (military MREs). Were we over-prepared? As it turned out we weren't. All communications were down and complete havoc surrounded us. Houses and road bridges were being washed away, mountain slopes were collapsing, and it was rumored that we were completely cut off from outside help. At the center we found space in a classroom with other evacuees. A few were clearly in a state of shock, having just lost their homes.

What struck me most was how ill-prepared they all were. Many had left their homes with minutes to spare. However, most people there had been given over an hour's warning time that they were going to be evacuated, as we were. And yet, they sat there dressed in sandals, shorts or jeans, and a T-shirt with a lightweight jacket. At their feet, some carried a small handbag. They had obviously brought nothing of any serious value for survival.

After a short while an official came into the room and told us they were going to evacuate us downtown to a school. I pointed out that the school was at the bottom of the valley, in a recognized flood zone. Plus, we would have to cross a bridge that some officials had reported was in danger of collapsing. The official replied that they had fresh water and coffee there with food, and that the school was closer to medical support at the hospital. He said it was worth the risk of crossing the bridge to get there.

My wife pointed out that fresh water was falling from the sky, and that we had food and medical supplies in our bags. In addition, she mentioned that she felt that it was not worth crossing a bridge at the risk of getting washed away—or of entering a flood zone on a day like today.

The official curtly replied that we had no choice and needed to go. My wife and I looked at each other, smiled, picked up our gear, and headed out the door. "We have every choice," we announced as the official screamed that we had to get on the bus. We secured the laces on our boots and headed off.

As I glanced back, I saw people lining up in the gray pouring rain to get on the bright yellow school buses. They meekly shuffled forward, like lambs, while officials circled and barked commands at them. All were underdressed and ill-informed, and willing to be led by the local authorities they believed were making the best decision for their safety.

It took a mere twenty-four hours for our modern town to come to a halt, with no water, no electricity, and shops depleted of food. Two weeks later we were still recovering and trying to get back to normal. A year later the roads and other services were still being repaired. We also found out that the gates of a major water reservoir above our town had been close to failing. At one location the escaping water from the reservoir had washed away parts of the valley railway. This potential catastrophic failure had been noticed by the authorities at the same time as they were shipping people in buses to the school evacuation center at the bottom of the valley. Thankfully those on the bus were lucky.

It's a dangerous world these days—floods, wildfires, and other potentially apocalyptic events will likely become more commonplace.

But you *always have a choice* when it comes to apocalyptic worst-case scenarios. You can sit there and hope they won't happen to you and complacently believe that your local authorities will guide you toward safety . . . or you can take steps to be prepared and learn what to do.

You can take courses in first aid and survival. You can stock up on emergency supplies and educate your family. And you can read this book. Though it's meant for entertainment and is at times tongue in cheek, *The Worst-Case Scenario Survival Handbook: Apocalypse* will help you face your fears when things take a turn for the worse. It's educational and entertaining—full of essential facts and hardline information that come from first-class experts in their fields.

The victims we were with in the evacuation center would have gained much from reading the chapter on How to Pack a Go Bag in Thirty Minutes, or How to Survive a Superflood.

I hope you enjoy the book, and learn a few things about surviving the apocalypse. Choose to be prepared, to be informed and remain calm, whether you're faced with likely situations such as floods and wildfires, or more unlikely scenarios such as robots or alien visitors.

You and your loved ones will be grateful you are even just a little bit ready to survive the worst.

And if aliens do eventually visit us, it will be good to know how to tell if they are coming in peace.

–Dave Holder,
Outdoor Leader and Wilderness Guide Instructor
at Mahikan Trails (mahikan.ca)

INTRODUCTION

"What the caterpillar calls the end of the
world, the Master calls the butterfly."

–Richard Bach, *Illusions*

"Don't panic."

–Douglas Adams,
The Hitchhiker's Guide to the Galaxy

Since 1999, Worst-Case Scenario Survival Handbooks
have been providing expert advice on surviving all
manner of extreme situations—alligator attacks, airplane
disasters, runaway trains, hotel fires, and many more
of life's sudden turns for the worse. After twenty-plus
years, we thought we had covered it all, helping millions
of people get comfortable with facing their fears in the
knowledge that no matter how bad things get, there are
always answers to be found—there are always ways to
survive the worst.

Then 2020 came—ushering in an era of existential
angst, a global pandemic, climate crises galore, civil
unrest, worldwide authoritarian threats, floods and
wildfires and impending nuclear disasters and wars and
more.

Lately, it seems like the doomsday clock is ticking ever closer to midnight.

But there are *always* ways to survive even the most apocalyptic of situations. Life, after all, has a way of finding a way to keep living—even if it involves eating insects and drinking urine.

At the end of the day, the three primary principles of survival hold true:

Be Prepared. Don't Panic. Have a Plan.

The Worst-Case Scenario Survival Handbook: Apocalypse can help you with all three—from How to Prep Your Bunker to How to Determine If Conditions Are Safe, from How to Survive an Alien Invasion to How to Defeat a Global Supercomputer, and from How to Fend Off Hostile Clans to How to Rebuild a Utopian Society, we hope you'll learn enough to feel that even when things take a turn for *the very worst* there are always going to be answers.

There will also be a lot fewer options for what to binge watch.

So, stay positive, survivors. Because we humans are pretty inventive and resilient, as long as we can work together. And after all, there's no *I* in *apocalypse*. But there is an *I* in *survive*.

We're not sure what that really proves, but darn it, it's got to mean something good.

–The Authors,
Joshua Piven and David Borgenicht

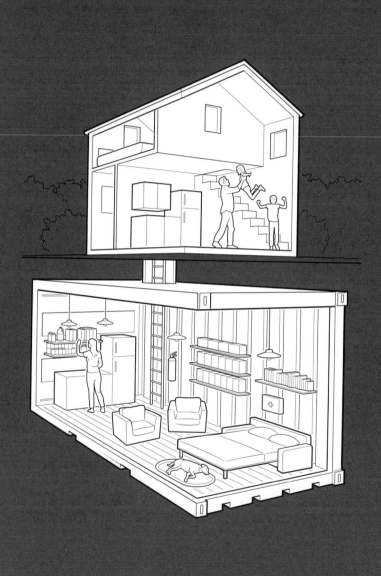

Being Prepared

HOW TO NOT PANIC WHEN YOU THINK THE WORLD IS ABOUT TO END

- **Keep hope alive.**

  We tend to assume that bad events will feel worse than they actually feel, and will impact us longer than they actually do (this is referred to as *impact bias*). Remain focused on the knowledge that *Homo sapiens* is highly evolved to adapt to new conditions and create favorable circumstances amidst even the worst of scenarios.

- **Embrace your worries and thoughts as data.**

  Resist the urge to assume that when bad things happen, you will be negatively impacted. You may be—you may not be. There is no way of knowing. Until then, your "psychological immune system" will help you in various ways: rationalizing, seeking social support, making you work harder, and so forth. While these responses happen unconsciously, take comfort in the knowledge that your brain is constantly processing new information and adjusting your behavior.

- **Normalize your negativity.**
  Being afraid (experiencing fear) may be effective in getting you out of danger, while sadness may indicate you are lacking some needed social or emotional support. Treat negative emotions as signals to act, which can help you survive when conditions get really bad.

- **Maintain control over your emotions.**
  There is always one thing completely under your control at all times: your reactions. Focus on controlling your reactions to bad situations, which will help engender a feeling of control and a more positive attitude. When we lack control, we experience feelings of helplessness and powerlessness. Research indicates the *perception* of control is a self-fulfilling prophecy that can help establish actual control over events.

- **Make jokes, notice beautiful things, and stay positive.**
  People can be happy in even the direst circumstances by controlling what they do and how they think. This is why people often make jokes when stressed or afraid—humor and joy short circuit fear and panic. Consider things you are grateful for, connect socially with others, take actions to help others, and do not lose your sense of humor or you are really and truly screwed.

- **Focus on positive habits—and avoid negative ones.**
  Exercise, meditation, and getting sufficient sleep tend to make people happier, even under difficult conditions. Eating poorly, worrying, drinking too much, or using drugs to alter your mood tend to make people less happy.

PRO TIP

Closing your eyes and simply taking three mindful, deep belly breaths can often be enough to alter your mood and clear your brain of anxious thoughts.

Use mindfulness to maintain control over your emotions.

HOW TO PACK A GO BAG IN THIRTY MINUTES

Your go bag is a portable, temporary bridge to a longer-term evacuation solution. Stock it with critical items to last several days, not weeks or months. Each family member save babies and toddlers should have their own bag. A suitable go bag is a waterproof duffle with a sturdy shoulder strap, not a hard-shelled "wheelie" suitcase with cheap plastic rollers.

1 **Gather phone numbers (minutes 1-5).**

Each go bag should contain a short, identical list of critical phone numbers, including family, close friends, or others you may need to contact. If and when your cell phone dies, you will rely on this list.

2 **Gather paperwork (minutes 6-10).**

Place passports, birth certificates, national identification cards (such as social security cards in the US), insurance policies, and other critical items in a large waterproof bag. Seal it shut, using tape if needed. (Images of all documents should be stored securely in the cloud as well.)

3 **Gather medications, first aid, and toiletries (minutes 10-15).**

If prescription drugs are needed, each family member should pack their own supply; a week's worth is recommended. Take this time to pack needed toiletries.

4 **Gather clothing (minutes 16-20).**

Each family member must have two changes of clothes, several pairs of socks and underwear, a warm coat, sturdy shoes, and a water-resistant jacket or portable poncho. A larger family bag should contain warm blankets.

5 **Gather these essential survival items (minutes 21-30).**

- ▶ One gallon of water per person per day
- ▶ Protein bars, nuts, peanut butter, beef jerky or other dried protein source
- ▶ Small flashlights with batteries
- ▶ Portable battery-powered radio
- ▶ Dryer lint (for starting fires)
- ▶ Lighter and matches in a waterproof pouch
- ▶ Water purification tablets
- ▶ Leatherman or other multi-tool
- ▶ Portable batteries for charging cell phones, plus cables
- ▶ Trash bags, duct tape, string or twine
- ▶ Small mirror, compass
- ▶ Work gloves

- ▸ Face masks (for filtering dust, ash, or contaminants)
- ▸ Toilet paper
- ▸ Pens and pencils
- ▸ Pet food (if applicable)

PRO TIPS

- ▸ Tarps or plastic sheeting are useful for creating shelter or keeping items dry. Store several in your car, along with a first aid kit.

- ▸ Establish an emergency meet-up location, in case you are separated and cell service is interrupted or overtaxed.

- ▸ Visit www.ready.gov/kit for a printable list of go bag items.

Gather these essential items:

toilet paper

1 gallon water

trash bags

duct tape

purification tablets

dryer lint

face masks

battery-powered radio

protein bars

small mirror and compass

portable battery

multi-tool

flashlight

pens and pencils

work gloves

lighter and matches

pet food

HOW TO APOCALYPSE-PROOF YOUR FINANCES

- **Go back to paper.**

  The global financial system is digital. With the exception of hard currency and gems or minerals (which have no intrinsic value on their own), all accounts, records, credits, debits, and investments are held electronically. In an apocalyptic event—or even a major cyberattack—records of your assets may be lost or inaccessible for long periods. To prepare, go online and print records of your investments and bank accounts at the end of each trading day. These will serve as proof of ownership later, should you need it.

- **Ensure you have an "air gap."**

  Dedicate a separate computer and printer to the process of collecting and printing your documents, located in a secure, fireproof room. Disconnect the computer from the internet (called air-gapping) when it's not in use to protect against cyberwarfare.

- **Avoid digital currency.**

  Bitcoin, Dogecoin, Ethereum, and the like do not exist as physical money. In the apocalypse, they will be inaccessible and worthless, and the energy-intensive mining system will collapse.

- **Hold some cash, but do not convert everything.**

  The US dollar and all other major currencies are independent of the gold standard and are essentially a promise to pay. In the early stages of the apocalypse, when the banking system is faltering, there will be bank runs and moves to cash, and dollars may continue to be accepted in place of credit. However, with time hard currency will likely become worthless as a barter and exchange economy re-forms. Keep whatever's left for starting fires.

- **Buy land, especially good farmland or timberland.**

  In a postapocalyptic feudal, agrarian, or preindustrial society, landowners will control both the means of production and, potentially, any housing stock that still remains. The more property you own, the more options you will have not only to evacuate, but to begin again with something of value. If you already own your home and/or land, keep good paper records of any deeds to prove ownership.

- **Consider mortgage options.**

  In a global apocalypse, banks and mortgage companies will disappear, so paying off your mortgage beforehand may be pointless: there will be no one left to foreclose on you. However, in a more temporary disaster, these organizations will almost surely bounce back after some period of instability and come for what you owe.

- **Hold some physical gold.**

  Gold is essentially indestructible and may be useful as barter early in the apocalypse, but less so as time passes. Though ancient civilizations valued gold—a soft metal—it was for ornamental, not practical, purposes. See How to Buy and Sell Gold, below, for details on purchase options and quality.

- **Stockpile barterable items.**

  Space permitting, use currency today to purchase things that will be useful in the coming apocalypse, such as solar chargers, portable batteries, water purifiers, seeds, coolers, axes and bush knives, and guns and ammunition. See How to Prep Your Bunker, page 34, for a full list. If you have room, raise chickens and rabbits.

- **Spend it all now.**

  Expect, and prepare today, to live simply later. Spend down most of your assets before the apocalypse. This will both minimize regret at what's been lost later and, once your possessions are mostly gone, provide necessary practice for living a more subsistence-based life.

HOW TO BUY AND SELL GOLD

- **Determine type of gold you have or need.**

  Physical gold bullion—either bars or coins—is generally purer, more desirable, and easier to exchange than gold items like jewelry (known in the trade as *scrap*, more below).

- **Determine brand.**

  Like many products, the "brand" (the producer or refiner) of the gold helps determine its value. Check the Good Delivery List from the London Bullion Market Association (LBMA) online for reputable producers and sellers.

- **Weigh the gold.**

  The most commonly traded gold bars and coins contain one Troy ounce of pure metal. But in Europe bars may be as large as 250 grams, and in the US coins may range from one-twentieth Troy ounce to one full Troy ounce. Bullion products typically have the type, weight, and purity stamped on them. Use a food scale if necessary to convert to Troy ounces (see below for conversion information).

- **Calculate value.**

  Most investment-grade bullion products are .999+ fine (equivalent to 24 karat jewelry). The closer to .999+, the better, although gold Eagles (minted in the US), which have a fineness of .9167, or gold Krugerrands (minted in South Africa), at .916 fine, are also widely accepted. Canadian-minted Maple Leaf coins are also well traded. Regardless of purity, keep in mind that gold prices fluctuate, sometimes considerably. During and after the apocalypse, gold may increase in value—or it may plunge, since it's primarily an ornamental metal with little practical use.

- **Buy or sell online if possible.**
  You will get the best prices online, where the market for gold is enormous and active. There are a number of reputable online precious metal dealers.

- **Go local.**
  Local brick and mortar dealers usually have some gold stock, but during a crisis their prices may be high and items may be unavailable.

- **Buy from the government.**
  This is generally the most expensive option—and of course you can only buy, not sell. National mints (United States Mint, Royal Canadian Mint) are sources of much of the world's supply of bullion products, so supply should be adequate, but expect higher prices.

If you only have scrap gold

Selling or bartering jewelry presents some challenges. Jewelry varies in purity from 10k to 24k, and without adequate assay tools and an accurate scale, determining value is difficult. Jewelry also comes in all shapes and sizes, from a 5 gram wedding ring to a thick gold chain that may weigh 200 grams. Gold jewelry also may contain gemstones, which must be removed. If you intend to buy or sell scrap gold, buy a basic assay kit, jeweler's tools, and a jeweler's scale online (all in all, this costs about $300) to help determine its value.

PRO TIPS

▶ Bullion bars and coins are measured in Troy ounces (not regular ounces), a unit of measure dating to the Middle Ages and Troyes, France. One Troy ounce equals just over 31.1 grams (a standard ounce is slightly less).

▶ The high value of even small amounts of gold presents its own set of challenges. Many everyday items are worth a lot less than a single Troy ounce. Consider buying a Monster Box of silver (500 coins/ounces, worth about $23/ounce at time of writing) or a bag of so-called junk silver (pre-1965 US coins containing about 90 percent silver) that can be used to acquire basic, inexpensive items.

HOW TO PREP YOUR BUNKER

TO BUILD

1   **Determine the length of your stay.**

A small, inexpensive bunker is appropriate for stays of
a few days to a month. Beyond that timeframe, storage,
power, air filtration, and water and waste issues make tiny
bunker life impractical.

2   **Select a concealable location for your bunker.**

Secret bunkers are secure bunkers. A backhoe operating
during daylight will draw nosy neighbors expecting a
swimming pool. If you have a basement, build a false
wall using cinderblocks. Cover with drywall. Conceal the
entry with a bookcase or shelving. This safe room should
be outfitted like a small apartment with beds, a kitchen,
and a basic bathroom. See below for infrastructure
requirements.

3   **Build out from basement.**

If you have sufficient land around your home and a small
basement, dig a tunnel through a foundation wall (with
appropriate support) and locate your bunker at the end

of it. Build a separate tunnel with a small generator room that is properly vented to the surface. This room should be used to store combustible fuel for the generator. Conceal the tunnel and the surface vent. Do not place your bunker under your neighbor's yard.

4 **Bury a shipping container.**

Used shipping containers are inexpensive (between $3,000 and $8,000 depending on size) and make good buried bunkers. You'll need to rent an excavator and a crane, and have enough land so the neighbors can't see what you're up to.

5 **Weatherproof the exterior, then create infrastructure for drainage and airflow.**

Waterproof the exterior with tar, asphalt shingles, or other material. Dig sufficient drainage channels around it. Line the drainage channels with rocks. You will need welding skills (or a discreet welder) to cut an opening in the top for a hatch and air pipes. The container should be at least ten feet underground and accessed via a concealed ladder and lockable hatch. You will need a separate space for a generator, as above.

Bury a shipping container and conceal beneath a tiny house for a simple and inexpensive bunker.

TO CONCEAL

- **Top with a tiny house.**
  Many people are adding tiny houses to their yards for extra living space, or to rent. Build a normal-looking tiny house over a hidden hatch that covers access to the bunker. Top the hatch with a tasteful rug.

- **Place bunker directly under garage.**
  Be prepared to jackhammer through the garage's cement floor to access the bunker ladder below.

- **Cover entrance with flower bed.**
  Build or buy a six-by-six-foot flower bed. Attach sturdy wheels to all four corners. Cover the gap with trim. Paint. Plant tasteful flowers. Roll the flower bed to the side to access the bunker hatch.

- **Hide with decking.**
  A deck can easily disguise the bunker hatch. Cut and hinge the section over the hatch, then hide this trapdoor with an outdoor rug. Sisal is durable and attractive.

PRO TIPS

- ▸ You can purchase a relatively inexpensive prebuilt shelter online: for one option, visit Atlas Survival Shelters (atlassurvivalshelters.com).

- ▸ If price is no object, you can invest in a prebuilt bunker home in an underground community in Kansas (survivalcondo.com). Prices begin at several hundred thousand dollars and go up to many millions, depending on square footage. These staffed and secure facilities are equipped for off-grid living for decades. A pool is included.

- ▶ You can buy and outfit an empty nuclear missile silo in many US states, including Arizona, Kansas, New Mexico, Oklahoma, and Texas. These FUDS (Formerly Used Defense Sites), owned by the US government, contain hardened Atlas F missile silos that are widely considered among the most fortified locations on Earth. Prices vary but start at around $250,000.

- ▶ Maintain a 30-day supply of drinking water for all inhabitants. You will need one-half to one ounce of water per pound of body weight, per person, per day.

  - Fill your bunker kitchen with foodstuffs to last 30 days or more. Grains are shelf stable for many months, canned goods for years.

  - Fortified bunkers have negative air pressure, preventing contaminants from entering. Your backyard bunker will not have this pricey system but should at least have good ventilation with HEPA and charcoal filters.

  - Use a composting toilet if you cannot connect to a nearby sewer line.

  - Keep a large stock of card games, board games, and 1,000-piece puzzles. A small library is also recommended.

  - Keep movies on hand for evening entertainment, if you have electricity and a means to watch.

- Space permitting, add a treadmill or stationary bike, weights, and a padded area for yoga and stretching.

- Consider an animal: Cats are bunker friendly. While some dogs can be bunker-trained, most need to be walked. Leave the bunker only at night or you risk being spotted. A fish tank may be an option, but most tanks require a constant supply of electricity, which may be at a premium in your bunker during the apocalypse.

HOW TO MAKE YOUR BUNKER FEEL LIKE HOME

1 **Use proper lighting.**

Install only LED lightbulbs with at least a 3000K rating to reduce the chances of seasonal affective disorder.

2 **Keep ceilings high.**

To reduce the natural feeling of claustrophobia associated with living underground, consider ceiling heights of nine feet in living and sleeping areas. Bathroom ceilings can be lower. In no case should the ceiling height be less than seven feet. Shipping containers typically used for bunkers are eight and a half feet high, eight feet wide, and forty feet long.

3 **Build LED "windows."**

Frame televisions or computer monitors so they look like windows. Mount them on walls and display photos of outdoor scenes.

4 **Use mirrors strategically.**

Mirrors give the illusion of space. While too many will make your bunker feel like a funhouse, a few carefully placed large mirrors will make your bunker feel larger than it is. Lucite tables will also help to make things feel more spacious.

5 **Position furniture away from walls.**

Furniture shoved directly against bunker walls will make your survival space feel cramped. Create seating pods toward the centerline of the bunker.

6 **Paint using light colors.**

In addition to white, light shades of blue, yellow, and green will soften hard surfaces, and tend to make people feel more relaxed. Dark colors will make the bunker feel small and should be avoided. Do not use red.

7 **Divide spaces without using walls.**

Open shelving can be used to separate dining and living areas without the need for full-height walls. Light-colored linen room dividers on ceiling tracks or folding screens that can be easily opened or closed are also good choices to demarcate separate areas.

8 **Reduce clutter.**

Storage is at a premium in a bunker. Use benches with interior storage for seating, and build platform beds with drawers underneath. Closets should be double hung.

BARTERABLE ITEMS TO STORE

The value of tradable goods will be determined by both the type of disaster at hand and the relative scarcity of particular items. Use the following as a rough guide to supplies that are likely to be sought after and that are easy to store for long periods.

- ▶ D-cell batteries, for powering radios and portable lights and lanterns
- ▶ Flashlights and radios
- ▶ Cooking gas or propane, for boiling water, cooking, and sterilization
- ▶ Water purification tablets
- ▶ Solar chargers, for phones and lights
- ▶ Goats, for milk, cheese, and meat (space permitting)
- ▶ Toilet paper
- ▶ Over-the-counter fever reducers such as aspirin
- ▶ First aid kits
- ▶ Bush knives
- ▶ Seeds
- ▶ Shelf-stable foods such as pasta, rice, and canned goods
- ▶ Chickens, for eggs and meat
- ▶ Tarps and ponchos
- ▶ Duct tape
- ▶ Rope

- Playing cards
- Rabbits, for meat and fur
- Chess sets
- Buckets and pails
- Pots and pans
- Charcoal
- Guns and ammunition
- Bulletproof vests
- Coloring books

HOW TO HIDE YOUR PREPAREDNESS

1 **Shop late at night, or online.**

Other shoppers may be suspicious if your cart is filled with fifty cans of Dinty Moore Beef Stew, two hundred pounds of rice, or twelve car batteries. Make multiple trips over time, or order in bulk online. Items delivered via forklift are sure to arouse suspicion.

2 **Avoid camouflage and flannel.**

Nobody is hunting you, and if you will be hunting, you can change later. Preppers favor durable brands like Carhartt, but consider Patagonia's more fashionable outerwear, which is well-made and long-lasting.

3 **Do not wear a utility belt.**

A heavy-duty belt with a Leatherman or other multi-tool, a sheathed buck knife, and bear spray may tip others off that you're a prepper. Most people now carry a cell phone in a pocket, not a belt pouch. Zip ties are scary.

4 **Use appropriate language.**

There's a fine line between reasonable preparation and prepping. Instead of saying "We will be the only ones left standing after a mass-extinction event," say "I think we'll be OK for a few days in a storm." If someone asks, "Why are you dehydrating fifty pounds of beef?" say "Would you like some jerky?"

5 **Do not use potential trigger words.**

Words and phrases like *ham radio*, *iodine tablets*, *dosimeter*, and *gas masks* are sure to make nonpreppers suspicious. *N95 mask* may now be used in casual conversation.

6 **Never ever show off your prepper pantry, safe room, or bunker.**

Resist the urge to brag about all your hard work, the money you've spent, how safe you feel, or how long you can hold out when it hits the fan. Preppers tend to believe they are smarter than the average person, so staying silent may be challenging.

HOW TO HIDE OUT IN THE WILDERNESS

In large areas of unpopulated federal wilderness, your chances of discovery are low—assuming nobody is looking for you. Check maps for national parks or other areas with few marked roads. (There is a listing of US wilderness areas by state at wilderness.net/default.php.) The six primary areas of concern before you leave are: first aid, fire, shelter, clothing, water, and food. (Food is less important since eventually you will harvest plants and catch and kill your protein; bring enough to last until you can hunt efficiently.)

1 **Prepare a pack that weighs no more than forty pounds.**

Bring the following items if they are not already in your go bag.

▶ Military-style poncho, large enough to be used as a shelter

▶ Leatherman Wave or other high-quality multi-tool

▶ Cranking portable transistor radio

- ▸ Small solar charger and a rechargeable flashlight with red or blue filter
- ▸ Watch and compass
- ▸ 8-inch folding saw
- ▸ Ferrocerium spark rod
- ▸ Mora carbon steel bush knife 4.3-inch blade, or similar from another high-quality brand (can also be used to create sparks)
- ▸ Small bush axe, carbon steel
- ▸ Water purification tablets
- ▸ Several disposable lighters and boxes of kitchen matches in sealable plastic bags
- ▸ Folding camping shovel
- ▸ Camping pot or pan
- ▸ Rope or twine
- ▸ Warm clothing and good shoes
- ▸ Insulated water bottle
- ▸ Clear water bottle (for ultraviolet purification)
- ▸ Nuts, dried fruit, and energy bars
- ▸ Dog food, as needed (your dog should carry)

2   **Hike in.**

Stay far away from travel lanes. For safety, hike into the woods at least half a mile from anything that even resembles a road, track, or trail. Even a seemingly disused fire road may be frequented by park rangers or hunters.

Do not attempt to cover your tracks with brush, as disturbed ground is easy to spot. Instead, walk on hard ground, preferably rocks or gravel.

3 **Pick a spot near a water source.**

A stream or creek should be close enough to hike to, but not so close that your homestead might attract visitors. Check mud, sand, and riverbanks for footprints or other signs of human habitation before you settle; recheck regularly. Use different routes to and from the water source to help avoid ambush.

4 **Practice carrying out tasks at night.**

Sit in the dark for thirty minutes to allow your eyes to adjust to night vision. Never use your flashlight without the filter. It reduces brightness and helps conceal your position. Unless absolutely necessary, use artificial light only in your shelter.

5 **Build a fire for heat and cooking—but only at night.**

Using the lighter, matches, or spark rod, build a fire with dry wood. Never build a fire during the day when the smoke might be spotted.

6 **Purify water.**

Boil any water and use purification tablets (see Dirty Water, page 170).

7   Regularly patrol your homestead.

Be prepared to patrol the area immediately around your shelter daily, looking for tracks or other signs of intruders. If you have a dog, it may be a useful sentry, as long as it does not give away your position by barking.

8   Set trip wires.

Pull the tops of live saplings across areas you traverse and tie down loosely with twine. If you hear the trees snap back, be ready to confront invaders. If trip wires may give away your location, alternatively scatter dry branches on the ground, which will crack under pressure and alert you to intruders, human or animal.

HOW TO RELOCATE TO ANOTHER COUNTRY

1 **Determine the length of your stay.**

Immigration rules vary by country, but most allow a stay of at least three months (and occasionally up to six months) without a residency visa or special work permit. Depending on the conditions in both home and foreign countries, consider traveling for several months as a tourist before undertaking a major move. An extended stay will also give you a sense of the people, culture, potential language challenges, and costs associated with living abroad.

2 **Check with an embassy or consulate.**

Relocating abroad is rarely simple or quick, even if you marry a foreign national. The US State Department recommends confirming specific visa and work and/or residency requirements of your target country several months before you plan to move. While there are some exceptions for Americans moving to Canada or Mexico, the process can be time-consuming and filled with paperwork. During a pandemic, added restrictions may make travel more difficult or impossible.

3 **Understand the tax implications.**

The US taxes on citizenship, not residency: you'll still need to file a tax return with Uncle Sam if you live abroad—unless you give up your citizenship. For this reason, many expats choose to work for US companies exclusively, so they don't also have to pay taxes to a second country. There are various credits and exclusions to avoid double taxation, so it's best to consult a specialist with expertise in this area before you move.

4 **Open a bank account.**

Paying bills in a foreign currency means you will need access to your funds. Depending on the country, you may be able to open the account online before you arrive. The bank may want proof of address to open an account, so you might need to find somewhere to live first. Consider making contacts through expat Facebook groups for the latest information and advice on which banks may be more lenient. Sign up for an online money transfer service, which lets you transfer money into different currencies at a low rate and maintain online accounts in different countries; use a debit card to make withdrawals in the local currency.

5 **Study healthcare and insurance options.**

As an expat, plan to get private international health insurance since most US insurers won't cover you if you move out of the country. (If you're working for a foreign company, you'll likely qualify for the country's national health service.) Private international insurance will provide access to better-equipped clinics in countries with poor medical infrastructure.

6 **Prepare your tech.**

WiFi is common in developed nations and populated areas. Check with your US cellular carrier to determine if your current phone will work on your target country's network; it may not, or adding service may be expensive. You'll likely move to a local carrier soon after arrival. A Google Voice number can be useful for forwarding calls from your US number or accessing messages on the web. WhatsApp and Signal allow free text messaging internationally.

PRO TIP

Local SIM cards are usually cheap. Choose a monthly or pay-as-you-go contract, if your plans are in flux. Some phones now support dual or virtual SIMs, so you can keep your US plan, but this probably won't be necessary unless you're only abroad for a short time.

HOW TO OBTAIN CITIZENSHIP

There are two primary means of securing citizenship in a different country: investment and descent, also known as citizenship by descent or CBD. Countries that allow visa-free travel to—and the ability to work in—many other nations (such as within all the European Union nations) are generally considered more desirable than those that do not.

Investment

Many countries will grant citizenship in return for a cash investment or real estate purchase, often for as little as around $100,000 for an individual (spouses and families cost more). During the COVID-19 pandemic, some countries created bond citizenship programs to raise money, where citizenship is granted in exchange for investment and then the applicant's funds are returned after a fixed number of years (at low or no interest). Countries differ on whether or not residency is required, and some will only grant citizenship following a long period of residency, so check local regulations.

The following counties had relatively affordable citizenship-for-investment programs at the time of writing:

▶ Antigua and Barbuda

▶ Bulgaria

▶ Dominica

- Germany
- Greece
- Grenada
- Ireland
- Malta
- Montenegro
- Portugal
- Spain
- St. Kitts
- Turkey
- Vanuatu

Ancestry

Most countries will grant citizenship to individuals who can document ancestors that were citizens of that nation, usually via birth certificates or other medical records. This is known as *jus sanguinis*, which is Latin for "right of blood."

Some countries will grant citizenship based only on parental citizenship, while others allow it based on the citizenship of grandparents. A few countries (Italy being the most well-known example) have no generational limit: if your great-great-great-great grandparent was a citizen, you can apply, as long as you have documentation, which may be difficult to obtain.

The list of nations that allow second-generation

CBD is long, and includes the US, most members of the European Union, most Scandinavian countries, and many nations in Asia and Africa. The number that allow third-generation CBD (that is, grandparents) is shorter, but includes Spain and Ireland, among others. Israel's Right of Return allows anyone of Jewish descent to apply for citizenship. Check the web for lists of countries that support jus sanguinis and their specific requirements, which may include speaking the language and various medical tests and certifications.

HOW TO SNEAK OVER A BORDER

- **Overstay your visa.**

  The easiest way to "sneak" into another country (and the method used most often) is to enter legally and then stay after you're required to leave. Note: Since this is illegal, you'll be deported if caught, unless granted asylum.

- **Do not fly or take the train.**

  Even if you have (convincing) false identification, facial recognition software will probably catch you at a legitimate checkpoint or border crossing. If you must attempt an open crossing at a border station, alter your appearance with a disguise such as glasses, facial hair, or a prosthetic nose.

- **Check maps.**

  Major roads that cross national borders typically have customs and immigration stations, with armed guards. Unless you're a stowaway, do not attempt to cross at or near these areas. Avoid tightly controlled and militarized borders, and those that are disputed or between hostile nations (North and South Korea, Russia and Ukraine).

- **Study terrain carefully.**

  Using Google satellite and terrain view, locate border regions that are both accessible and easy to cross. Check elevations. Mountainous terrain may be remote, but dangerous without proper training and supplies; deserts may be flat and sparsely populated but too hot (and filled with venomous snakes). Rivers may be too rapid. Avoid nations with very small borders, which are easily patrolled.

- **Monitor potential crossing point several days ahead of planned departure.**

  From a safe location, study the border. Learn patrol schedules, check for technology (cameras, radar, infrared imaging), and watch for others who may be crossing at your chosen location. Keep in mind that illegal immigrants may be caught miles from their points of crossing.

- **Gather supplies.**

  Assume you will be without access to food, water, and shelter for several days. Monitor the weather and dress appropriately.

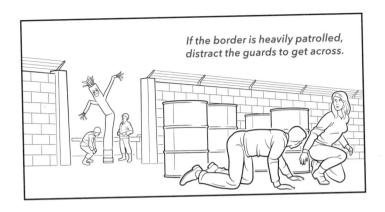

If the border is heavily patrolled, distract the guards to get across.

- **Create a diversion.**

  If you must cross in a heavily patrolled area, a car fire or other mishap may draw nearby border guards temporarily. Note, however, that it may also draw reinforcements.

- **Consider a bribe.**

  Private homes or businesses adjacent to border areas are often used by smugglers and criminal syndicates, either as departure points or tunnel entrances and exits. Offer a cash payment to a property owner to access a crossing point. This option should only be considered as a last resort.

- **Cross.**

  Depart based on the level of patrol activity and technology at your crossing point. Do not assume you are less likely to be spotted at night.

Apocalyptic Events

HOW TO SURVIVE AN ALIEN INVASION

IF THEY APPEAR FRIENDLY

Lack of immediate destruction is a positive sign. Take the following steps to prepare for negotiations and communication.

1 **Establish a shared frame of reference.**

Once you have determined the ETs have the desire and ability to communicate, establish labels for things and actions. Give examples that correspond to concrete objects, actions, properties, and spatial or temporal orientations, as you would when teaching someone a foreign language. Start with simple questions such as "Welcome, friends, where do you come from?" and "What kind of food do you eat?"

2 **Build trust.**

You will not know the aliens' intentions or purpose in visiting Earth. The visitors may just be out of fuel, or they may be probing for weakness or checking blood type. With no history of either trust or distrust, assume the best at the outset of negotiations.

3 **Remain positive.**

Remember, the aliens could very well be here to help human civilization, offering cures for disease, quick fixes for climate change, or ways to destroy social media.

4 **Do not hold a grudge.**

Resist the urge to retaliate when things go wrong, as they inevitably will. If the aliens incinerate, say, a thousand people during their Earth landing, it may have been an accident. Retaliation will result in an act-react cycle, leading to a conflict spiral and possible Armageddon. Show forgiveness but be firm that more mass killings are not acceptable.

5 **Remain predictable.**

Do not attempt to keep the aliens off-balance through trickery, threats, bluster, or impossible demands. Be clear and consistent in your messaging. Do not assign the visitors "fun" nicknames such as Lollipop Head or Tommy Tentacles.

6 **Be prepared to give something up.**

Effective agreements often result when both parties finally choose to make a difficult sacrifice to prove they are acting in good faith—the so-called fail-safe option. Should a sacrifice become necessary to secure peace, consider, in this order: politicians, reality TV stars, lawyers, wealth managers.

IF THEY APPEAR HOSTILE

1 **Remain calm.**

As when facing any adversary, keep your wits about you and do not act rashly. Focus on your immediate safety (not being vaporized) before worrying about potential longer-term challenges (human organ harvesting).

2 **Seek shelter.**

Stay at home, moving to the basement if available, or an interior room away from windows.

3 **Stay quiet.**

Do not make excessive noise, as the aliens may have highly attuned hearing and might use sound to locate your position.

4 **Turn off air conditioners. Turn on heat.**

Aliens using infrared will use heat differential to locate humans. Keep your hideout as close to body temperature as possible.

5 **Monitor radio broadcasts.**

Radio transmissions—either civil and government or amateur—will be your best, and possibly only, source of information about the aliens: where they are, how they travel, who is being targeted, potential weaknesses, and any defense being mounted. If you hear only static, the aliens have jammed radio waves and are technologically advanced. You may be in serious trouble.

6 **If you are face to face with a hostile alien, go for areas of vulnerability.**

They may not have humanoid appearances, but in general sensitive regions include open orifices, eyes, gills, and gonads. Punch, poke, or prod these regions.

7 **Look for other sensitivities.**

Aliens may have hypersensitivity to light, sound, heat or cold, liquids, or other environmental conditions that differ from their home worlds. Turn on or off lights, music, sprinklers, and so forth to test their sensitivities. Pay close attention to their reactions to such changes. You may discover their Achilles' heel.

8 **Move only when it is safe.**

Once you have determined it is relatively safe to leave your shelter, gather family members, pets, and emergency supplies and travel to a more hardened location such as a designated shelter or bunker. If possible, travel in a large group (herd), which may give you some extra time to escape death rays if the aliens initially target weaker or slower members.

*Tails and tentacles can be difficult to conceal,
so look for unusual appendages.*

HOW TO SPOT AN ALIEN POSING AS A HUMAN

1 **Observe their gait.**

It is easy to appear human, but more difficult to walk naturally like one. Watch for unsteadiness, odd swinging of arms, or feet shuffling. If possible, observe from a protected location. When they think nobody is looking, the aliens may revert to their native style of movement, such as hopping, crawling, or slithering.

2 **Try to spot a tail or tentacle.**

These large appendages are difficult to hide under pants, especially jeans or yoga pants—such appendages must frequently be hidden under baggy clothing, trench coats, and costumes. Tail or tentacle = alien.

3 **Test them.**

Unless they've carefully studied human history, the aliens are unlikely to pass a simple verbal quiz. Ask, "Where were french fries invented?" "Was Rome built in a day?" or "Who was Millard Fillmore's vice president?" If they don't answer "Belgium," "No, it wasn't," or "Fillmore didn't have a vice president," they are an alien.

4 **Trick them.**

While having coffee with a suspected alien, casually note, "This coffee is pretty good. But don't you think it would be much richer with human blood?" Observe their reaction.

5 Make them think you are an alien, too.

Say "Let's find a hotel room and get out of these itchy human skins!" If they agree, do not go to the hotel room.

If they turn out to be a lizard

- **Watch for shedding.**

  All reptiles shed their skins or scales as they grow, called molting or sloughing. During this period, the aliens may become itchy and irritable, and more vulnerable to attack.

- **Keep them on ice.**

  Lizards require heat to regulate their body temperature. Lead the aliens into a hockey rink, meat locker, or overly air-conditioned office. When they become chilled and lethargic, overpower them and take control.

- **Intimidate.**

  Proffer a snakeskin belt or lizard-skin briefcase. Show it off, then say, "Friend of yours?"

- **Attack their young.**

  Most lizards lay eggs, making their offspring defenseless and especially vulnerable. While the aliens will surely protect their mating grounds, you may be able to kill them before they hatch.

- **Avoid mating.**

  Assuming it is physically possible, copulation results will be unpredictable.

HOW TO PILOT AN ALIEN CRAFT

1 Perform a preflight physical inspection.

No matter how technologically advanced it is, the alien ship will have some form of propulsion. Circle the fuselage to make sure nothing is obstructing the engines, and that they are undamaged. Check landing gear (and wheels, if present) for integrity and remove any pins located in the struts. Other pins may be in the ejection seats and canopy jettison handles, to prevent inadvertent retraction or deployment while parked. The pins will have obvious markings or streamers. Check windscreen for cracks. If the ship is not saucer-shaped and has wings, they should be mechanically sound. Dispatch any aliens, if necessary.

2 Enter cockpit.

In the cockpit or cabin, locate the pocket checklist (PCL), a reference document with the proper sequence for all ground and inflight operations, including engine start-up. Look for a card stowed in a seat pocket. It's unlikely the card will be printed in English. However, the symbols or letters printed on the PCL should match what you see next to the corresponding flight controls, giving you a general sense of the order of operations. Even advanced ships with fully digital displays should have manual backup gauges for the "six pack" of critical flight instruments (more on this below).

3   **Turn on battery.**

Military aircraft do not require keys for starting. The first button referenced on the PCL should correspond to a battery or master rocker switch. Turn it on. Lights on the panel will illuminate and gauges will come to life.

4   **Open fuel lines.**

Look for a rocker switch on the bottom left of the control panel to engage boost pumps and allow fuel flow. If the switch is not apparent, remember that the aliens may use their feet, tongue, or tentacles to operate the craft, so search other areas of the panel.

5   **Activate APU.**

A switch very close to the throttle turns on the auxiliary power unit that provides supplementary power to start the main engine.

6   **Start engine(s).**

This should be the next item on the start-up list. There may be one button for each engine, or one button for multiple engines.

7   **Move the throttle to idle.**

Push the throttle (basically, the control for propulsion) forward to the first detent. The throttle might be just to your left and slightly above your mid-thigh and slightly to the side, resting near your left hand (the alien's left pincer). (The throttle is always on the left in a tandem cockpit setup.) The stick or yoke, however, will be either between the legs or on the right—or possibly anywhere else, if the alien is tentacled.

8 **Establish location of critical flight instruments.**

Regardless of their level of technological advancement, the alien ships will still most likely follow the laws of physics. The pilot of the ship will rely on six key gauges, the "six pack," during flight:

- ▶ Airspeed indicator

- ▶ Attitude indicator

- ▶ Altimeter

- ▶ Heading indicator

- ▶ Vertical speed indicator

- ▶ Turn indicator

These instruments will be front and center on the control panel, whether digital or analog. In a heads-up display, they will be projected onto the windscreen and will be visible at all times.

9 **Locate control stick or yoke.**

The movement of the ship in flight will be controlled by a stick between your legs (assuming a single seat) or possibly a yoke (basically, the steering wheel) if there are tandem controls.

10 **Accelerate.**

Move the throttle to full forward or firewall. You will hear the propulsion system get louder. The ship will either roll forward or begin moving up and away. If it has flaps, these can safely be ignored; as you gain speed, air traveling across the ship naturally creates lift and the craft will "want" to become airborne on its own.

11 **Take off.**

Aim for a takeoff speed of 150 KIAS (knots indicated airspeed), though reading the alien airspeed indicator is unnecessary. You should notice the ground effect as the ship bumps or jitters a few feet off the ground, ready to fly. Slowly pull back on the stick or yoke and the craft should become airborne and rapidly gain altitude. Raise landing gear to reduce drag and make the ship more maneuverable.

12 **Maintain control.**

A spacecraft (human-made or otherwise) is capable of phenomenal airspeeds. Due to the rapid movement of air across the wings, only small adjustments of the stick are needed to change direction and altitude.

13 **Level off.**

Bring the throttle back to midrange and lower the nose so it is level with the horizon. This will help preserve fuel. Keep the ship level most of the time unless pursuing alien attackers, avoiding pursuit, or streaking low to attack ground targets.

How to attack

1 **Choose weapons systems.**

The alien spacecraft will likely have multiple types of offensive capabilities but, minimally, air-to-air and air-to-ground ordnance: lasers (likely), photon torpedoes, short-range infrared (heat-seeking) missiles, or laser-controlled bombs and missiles. Look for switches or buttons on the top left of the control panel or digital display with symbols or pictographs corresponding to *A/A* and *A/G*. There may also be buttons for the various weapons present on or directly next to the stick.

2 **Arm weapons.**

A master arm or safety switch, highlighted with yellow and black slashes, may also be present. If it's there, flip this switch from safe to arm, which may require two motions (pull out and up, pull out and down, and so on).

3 **Target.**

Once weapons are active, crosshairs will appear on the windscreen or digital display, similar to those on video games. Using the stick, steer the craft so enemies are within the targeting sights. Ships need not be precisely bull's-eyed in order to effectuate a kill.

4 **Fire.**

Pull the trigger on the stick to engage air-to-air weapons (missiles, lasers) or press a button for air-to-ground bombs. Repeat until the weapon is exhausted.

PRO TIPS

▶ Any ship requiring telekinesis to control should be destroyed, unless a kidnapped alien can be "convinced" to fly it for you.

▶ If labels are indecipherable (or missing), use trial and error to determine switch and control functions: just point and shoot.

▶ If any controls do not behave as expected, determine their function through trial and error. (No matter how tempting, do NOT press the big red button unless you have tried all other alternatives first.)

HOW TO OUTWIT A ZOMBIE HORDE

FAST MOVING

- **Use narrow alleys.**

  The less room there is to maneuver, the slower the horde will be. Look for narrow alleys and doorways than can only accommodate one person (or zombie) at a time. This will create a funnel effect where too many zombies cram in at once and block the progress of the horde behind.

- **Escape by boat.**

  Zombies cannot swim, and in all likelihood cannot work a kayak paddle or steer a canoe. Choose a boat with both motor and sail and visit the coast only to resupply.

- **Escape in a car.**

  Zombies move fast, but not that fast: they cannot outrun a vehicle. Avoid self-driving features that may cause the car to stop if it senses pedestrians, even undead ones.

- **Seek higher ground.**

  If you cannot find a vehicle, move to a high floor of a tall building, preferably by using the elevator. Then, move the elevator to the stop position to prevent the cab from going down. (Zombies are unlikely to understand how an elevator works, but don't take any chances.)

- **Barricade stairwells.**

  Force the zombies to use an outside approach. Like ants and other insects, the zombies may create a vertical bridge or rope of sorts, climbing up and over one another on the exterior of the building. However, with no handholds they will probably fall off, or you can pick them off one by one from above.

SLOW MOVING

- **Stay silent.**

  Zombies, like cats, are startled by loud noises. They may lumber toward the source of the sound. If you must speak, whisper. Otherwise, use hand signals. The more zombies that arrive, the more noise they will make, which will attract yet more zombies.

- **Create a distraction.**

  Leave a loud radio playing to attract the horde.

- **Run.**

  It's easy to outrun a stumbling horde, but you will tire before the zombies do; eventually, they'll catch up. Run toward an appropriate shelter, vehicle, or escape route.

- **Trap them.**

  Lead the zombies into muck or deep mud, which should slow them down for a while.

- **Use a decoy.**

  Depending on the nature of the virus, the zombies may eat or at least attack their own. If you can, capture and restrain a zombie, then use it as bait to distract the horde while you make your escape. Note: This will not fool them for long.

PRO TIPS

- ► Choose a defensive location with as few fronts as possible, such as a high mountain redoubt with steep cliffs. This will allow you to focus your defenses on one or two fronts.

- ► If you make it to an island, be aware that any infection introduced will spread rapidly. Quarantine new arrivals immediately and watch for signs of illness or zombification.

- ► Decapitation is generally effective in disabling the undead. The detached head, however, may continue to bite for some minutes.

HOW TO SURVIVE IF A FAMILY MEMBER IS BITTEN

- **Check their eyes.**

  Black, dead "shark" eyes indicate the family member is infected with a rage virus, flesh-eating, and out for blood. Red or bloodshot eyes indicate insensate zombies, while bleary white eyes indicate your loved one has been dead for a while, is fragile, and may fall apart if hit hard enough. Be gentle with them.

- **Do not attempt to reason.**

  Zombies are immune to reason, logic, or love. While they have good hearing, communicating will be challenging. Questions such as "Honey, are you sure you're feeling

OK?" or "Are you the flesh-eating type?" are unlikely to elicit a response.

- **Buy time.**
  Zombies are strong but dumb. Coax the zombified family member into a room or shed from which they will be unlikely to escape. This will give you some time to plan.

- **Prevent your loved one from seeing other zombies.**
  Move the family member into a garage or basement with no view, in case a group of other zombies stumbles past. If your family member is non-flesh-eating and just stupefied, consider placing a television in the room for distraction. Do not rile them up by showing them the news or any horror films.

- **Wait for an antidote.**
  The undead do not die, so time is on your side here.

HOW TO DEFEAT A GLOBAL SUPERCOMPUTER

1 **Air-gap everything.**

Any device connected to the web, from phone to lightbulb to WiFi refrigerator, is a potential entry point into your life. Get rid of all web-enabled gear, as well as any device (such as a basic cable-connected television) that may be vulnerable to hacking over a backend computer network.

2 **Unplug anything nonessential.**

The global supercomputer will seize power stations and transmission lines and may send electromagnetic pulses to fry any "dumb" device it cannot directly control using data. If possible, connect essentials such as a refrigerator to a discrete, local power source like an off-grid solar array or generator.

3 **Speak only to people you know to be actual people.**

Bots and chat bots, based on machine learning and drawing on infinite data sets, will be used to confuse,

Attack the computer's power supply, disable its controller, or use an EMP device seeded with a virus to disable.

EMP-like device (inside cake)

persuade, and manipulate humans, much like Facebook. Even without your specific data, the bots and algorithms will have sufficient general knowledge of humans *like* you to trick you into doing their bidding.

4 Test for AI by posing complex, conditional questions.

Ask questions that require abstract thought and cannot be easily answered with "yes" or "no." For example, don't say "You sound like a bot. Are you a bot? Please just tell me!" Instead, say "Think about someone very influential in your field. Don't tell me who it is, just describe their appearance, then tell me what the world would be like if this person had never existed." Or "Is chili better with beans or without? Why or why not?"

5 Avoid dating sites.

Matches are made via algorithms, and a supercomputer may attempt to manipulate matches to increase the odds that any babies born will have genetic traits favorable to the computer (for example, children who grow up to be art history majors, not engineers).

6 Feign incompetence/stupidity.

Play dumb to train the supercomputer to underestimate human abilities, allowing you to attack when the time is right. In similar fashion, attempt to poison the well via sabotage, giving the AI poor or misleading learning examples that will trick it into making bad decisions.

7   **Plan to attack the supercomputer power supply.**

Even in the future, the supercomputer will require power to operate and a means to stay cool, and even robust batteries eventually require recharging. Locate the AI's power and/or transmission source and disable or destroy it. Keep in mind the supercomputer will have already infinitely gamed this scenario: it will have hardened its defenses and may utilize a power source humans also require—a nuclear reactor, for instance—making sabotage too risky or potentially catastrophic.

8   **Attack and disable the supercomputer's controller.**

If it's not completely self-governing, the global supercomputer will likely be manipulated by either a bad state actor or a powerful corporation or group of corporations. While it may have some decision-making autonomy, the machine's creators will have knowledge of its design and will ultimately be the weak link. Consider planting a mole within the controlling organization who can sabotage the AI with a computer virus.

9   **Design a Trojan Horse or honeypot attack.**

The supercomputer will attempt to disable any conceivable threat, especially an electromagnetic pulse generator. Build a seemingly real EMP weapon seeded with malicious code or a virus that will infect the AI when it attacks.

HOW TO FIGHT A ROBOT UPRISING

- **Slow with oil, then incinerate.**

  Battle-bot infantry, even advanced military-grade tech, still requires traction to advance. Spray formations with aerosolized oil to slow them down, then ignite them using incendiaries or a flamethrower. Depending on heat tolerances, this may slow but not stop the robots.

- **Disable with sand.**

  Using large industrial fans, airborne crop dusters, or drones, spray fine-grain aerosolized sand at robot battle units. Even battle-hardened military robots will have moving parts that can be impeded (if not stopped completely) with sand particles. See How to Disable a Robot, below, for details.

- **Spray with sticky foam.**

  Blast the robots with expanding foam insulation. The stickiness will slow them down, and as the foam hardens they will become disabled. Foam is a close-range weapon, so be judicious and covert in your attack.

- **Use an electromagnetic pulse generator to confuse robotic electronics.**

  An electromagnetic pulse may disable or confuse current robot technology, though its effectiveness will vary depending on robotic defenses.

- **Counterattack using cyborgs.**

  Though not battle-hardened machines, cyborgs may have enhanced vision and hearing, data gathering and processing, and weapons systems far surpassing what humans can currently do on their own. In combination with drones or drone swarms, humans augmented with computer implants, while not robots, may provide a final line of defense. However, implanted tech may also be prone to hacking by the robots or their AI "brain."

PRO TIPS

- ▶ Battlefield drones carrying high explosives have already proved to be formidable weapons against armor and mechanized infantry.

- ▶ Tiny, self-correcting drones carrying projectiles or high explosives that swarm a target—so-called *slaughterbots*—are virtually impossible to stop.

- ▶ As a last resort, a final off-Earth retreat to the Moon or Mars may be required (though the tech for this trip will itself be vulnerable to AI attacks).

HOW TO DISABLE A ROBOT

1   **Cut its power source.**

All robots require some type of energy source to operate: electricity primarily, but in some cases gasoline, diesel fuel, or solar. Locate the fuel source and disconnect or damage it. It will likely be located centrally—in the robot's chest or central cavity.

2   **Remove the robot's propulsion system.**

Most robots have moving parts, even if they remain stationary. Check for hydraulic cylinders and disconnect lines, remove gearing, or damage joints at critical areas (hands, legs, arms). Large robots working in factories are likely to be well-hardened and may require tools (wrenches, pliers) to disable.

3   **Use sand or metal.**

Toss sand into the robot's moving parts. This may not destroy the robot but it should slow it down. Small ball bearings will also foul moving parts.

4   **Use tar.**

Tar is sticky and dries hard. Few current robots will survive an encounter with tar. Feathers are unnecessary.

5   **Soak the robot.**

Virtually no current robots are completely waterproof. Blast the robot with a hose or lure it into a pool or hot tub. Salt, which is corrosive, may also be added.

To fend off robots:

Remove power source.

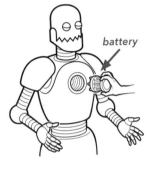

battery

Disable movement.

propulsion
system

**Use sand or oil to disable,
slow, and damage gears.**

**Soak with water to
damage electronics.**

sand

oil

water

▶ Small flying robots (drones) may be especially difficult to destroy, unless you can reach the human operator. Birds of prey have been known to attack quad-rotor drones. Keep an eagle or hawk on hand.

▶ Current robots have difficulty with stairs and may be tricked into a tumble. New technologies will likely overcome this obstacle in short order.

HOW TO DEFEAT ROBOTIC DOGS

Militarized robotic dogs are hardened with steel or titanium, so sticks, rocks, and low-caliber weapons will not put them down. Because they are designed to be waterproof or highly water-resistant, soaking will probably not be effective either. Take the following steps when tracked or attacked.

- **Disable the dog(s).**

  Toss thick netting over the dog from above, entwining its legs. Once the dog cannot maneuver, spray with sticky foam.

- **Climb a ladder.**

  Robodogs can climb stairs and maneuver on rocky or uneven ground, but are unlikely to be able to climb ladders. Use a tall ladder to move to a roof, then travel along rooftops.

- **Use a blinding light or strobe to confuse laser radar (lidar).**

  The dogs will likely use a combination of laser radar, standard radar, and cameras to navigate. Use a blinding dazzler weapon, if available, or a simple strobe to emit flashes of light that will disorient and temporarily blind the dog. A radar jammer may also be effective. Note that the robodog will have navigational redundancies, so jamming one system may not render it defenseless.

- **Use flares or heat to confuse infrared sensors.**

  Advanced, militarized robots will almost certainly use infrared sensors to detect heat differentials and pinpoint your position. Toss flares or use stationary fires, either to attract the dogs and then disable them or to camouflage your position. If trapped inside, turn the heat up.

- **Lure the robodogs to the beach.**

  The robodogs may have difficulty chasing you (or at least moving fast) in deep sand, giving you time to escape. While water is unlikely to disable them, they will not be fast swimmers—or buoyant—so you can swim to safety.

PRO TIPS

▶ Keep hands and fingers away from the robodog's joints to avoid being seriously injured.

▶ Depending on its level of autonomy, you may be able to disable a robotic dog by using a WiFi jammer, available online, to interrupt the signal from remote handlers.

HOW TO SURVIVE A SUPERFLOOD

FROM RISING RIVERS AND SEAS

Even if carbon emissions decline precipitously over the next eighty years, seas will continue rising. If a predicted one- to two-foot rise in sea levels occurs by 2100, storm surges will become massively more destructive. Eventually, insurance for at-risk regions will be eliminated or prohibitively expensive, and hard-hit areas may be abandoned to the ocean.

1 **Prepare for the flood.**

In most regions, keep a two- to three-day stock of emergency supplies on hand (in coastal regions, a week or more is recommended). Supplies should include bottled water and/or a purification kit; canned food items; a battery-powered radio; a camping stove and sufficient fuel; flashlights; and tarps or tents. A small boat may be useful for evacuations.

2 **Assess your danger level.**

While coastal areas may be inundated, areas near the coast may remain viable if infrastructure remains. If you are located within a one-mile zone of the coast, your area will be at grave risk of complete destruction.

3   **Avoid flood-prone regions.**

Several areas of the continental United States are likely to become uninhabitable within this century. Cities such as New Orleans (which is sinking), Houston, Miami, and Miami Beach are at high risk of repeated catastrophic flooding from storm surges. Most states along the Gulf Coast—especially coastal regions of those places—are also in the danger zone. While New York and Boston are likely to be inundated regularly as seas rise, these cities may have sufficient resources to build flood barriers to protect infrastructure. Barrier islands should be avoided.

4   **Watch for passing icebergs.**

In a catastrophic melting scenario, ice sheets will collapse and fall from land into the oceans. Antarctica alone holds enough ice to raise global sea levels by about two hundred feet (Greenland's ice sheet holds less). The resulting massive icebergs (likely to be hundreds of miles wide) will break apart and be carried across the globe by ocean currents and are likely to melt over several months or a year, raising seas by several inches. If you see an iceberg, prepare to migrate.

5   **Migrate.**

In the United States, move to interior or northern states in the Midwest (Nebraska, Kansas, Illinois, Minnesota) or western areas of eastern states (Pennsylvania, Virginia,

New York, Massachusetts). While these places may be less affected by sea level rise, they are still vulnerable to other dangers such as hurricanes and tornadoes. (Rivers may also rise and flood surrounding regions.) Noncoastal Canada is also a good choice to avoid rising seas.

FROM SUPERSTORMS

1   **Monitor forecasts.**

Weather forecasters are usually able to predict *where* it will rain but are less effective in accurately predicting rain amounts. Listen for terms like *flood warning* and *severe storm warning*, which indicate that dangerous weather is imminent, and be prepared to act.

2   **Listen.**

Dangerous rainstorms are usually accompanied by strong winds that may sound like a jet engine or a freight train.

3   **Watch for flying debris.**

Whether straight-line or rotating, strong winds will pick up and hurl objects at deadly speeds.

4   **Move to a higher floor.**

Basements and first floors may flood with little or no warning when sewers are overwhelmed during superstorms. Take shelter in an interior room on a higher floor. Avoid windows.

5 **Call for help.**

If you suspect imminent flooding, dial emergency services (911 in the US) and report your location. This will help direct first responders once rescue is possible.

6 **Evacuate if ordered to do so.**

Driving may be difficult or impossible, and you risk being carried away by floodwaters. Leave and move to higher ground only if you believe your location will be submerged.

HOW TO SURVIVE WILDFIRES

In a wildfire, the safest place to be is often an area that has already burned, what firefighters call in the black. If you are in the black, carefully consider any decision to leave it, especially if you are considering going into an area with unburned vegetation, also known as fuel. If you must move, take the following steps.

1 **Determine wind direction.**

Observe smoke carefully to see which way it is being blown. Look as high in the sky as possible, where smoke direction is less affected by contours in the terrain or pockets of intense heat on the ground. Watch carefully for strong rotation in the smoke plume above the fire. If you observe rotation, this indicates potential formation of a large fire whirl or firenado. When firenadoes form, they may move independently of the main fire and create massive damage from rotational winds.

2 **Determine slope.**

If you have the option, travel downslope. Hot air masses created by intense wildfires rise, and fires tend to spread more quickly uphill and burn hotter, making higher elevations more prone to ignition and more dangerous. Valley areas are more likely to hold moisture and contain less-combustible vegetation.

3   **Search for a firebreak.**

As you travel, look for a firebreak: paved or gravel roads, open meadows, clear-cut areas, right-of-ways (look for powerlines), boulder fields, or bodies of water. These areas may provide temporary safety from heat and flames until help arrives. Large rock outcroppings can also shield you from the heat emitted by the fire. As firefighters hike to a fire line, they are aware of LCES: lookouts, communication, escape routes, and safety zones. Sometimes the best escape route may be the route you've already traveled.

4   **Stay low.**

Low-lying areas with retained moisture may be safer than exposed hills and ridges.

5   **Move quickly.**

Wind-driven wildfires or fires burning up hills can move many times faster than a person can run, so use a vehicle if one is available. If you are on foot and fear you are being overtaken, cover exposed skin with dry clothing and seek a safe path through the leading edge of the fire into an area that has already burned. Drop any unnecessary gear or personal items. Keep lifesaving tools like your water bottle, trowel or tool for clearing debris, and navigation and communication devices.

Wildfires tend to head uphill, where combustible materials are drier.

Head toward low-lying areas (valleys and rivers) that will retain more moisture and resist combustion.

6 **Dig a fire trench.**

If you are surrounded and have no means of escape, move to an area of depression in the surrounding ground. Dig a hole in the side of the slope, place a tarp or blanket over the hole, cover it with dirt, and then crawl under the tarp into the hole. Alternatively, dig a trench two to three feet deep, lay down in it with your feet facing in the direction of the flames, and cover yourself with dirt. Leave an air hole, and wait for the fire to travel over you. Avoid gullies or chutes that are oriented down the hill; these tend to channel hot air and fire upward.

PRO TIPS

- ▶ Do not cover your mouth with a wet cloth: the superheated air from a wildfire may make breathing difficult or impossible, but dry air is less dangerous to the lungs than wet air.

- ▶ The coolest air is nearest to the ground. If you are caught and have only seconds to act, lay face down on the ground with your feet facing the oncoming fire. Dig a small depression for your face so you can breathe, and cover your back with any coats or extra clothing.

HOW TO PROTECT YOUR HOME FROM A WILDFIRE

1 **Choose a location near a fire hydrant.**

If you have the option before purchasing a home, choose a property as close to a hydrant as possible. Not only will water pressure be highest at this location, but firefighters will pay particular attention to the area around the fireplug to keep their equipment safe from the flames.

2 **Use Class A roofing material.**

Most fires spread via embers, which tend to land on roofs first as they travel on the wind. Common Class A roofing materials are tested against severe fire conditions, and include metal, asphalt-fiberglass composition shingles, concrete, and tiles. Your roof should be composed of one of these materials and clear of any dry foliage from trees.

3 **Keep your roof clean.**

Clear roof and gutters regularly, removing all combustible material including leaves, branches, and pine needles. Cut back any tree branches to ten feet or more from roof line.

4 **Clear brush.**

Remove dry or dead vegetation frequently. Maintain a noncombustible perimeter of at least ten feet from the exterior of the home; greater is safer. Do not plant trees or grasses that are naturally dry and highly combustible, such as eucalyptus or bamboo. Remove branches of any trees to a height of six to ten feet above ground level.

Tress with thicker trunks may take longer to combust than thinner ones, depending on climate conditions.

5 **Cover all vents.**

Embers may enter the home through ungrated vents (such as dryer vents) and uncapped chimneys. Protect all openings to the interior with metal capping or mesh.

6 **Remove or replace wooden fencing.**

Fire will travel along fences, which typically span the border between properties and are often attached to the exterior of homes. Replace wooden fences with metal or fire-resistant material such as vinyl (though it's also combustible), particularly if the fence is touching the home itself.

7 **Avoid wood siding.**

Wood siding and shingles will readily combust. The exterior of the home should be a fire-resistant material such as brick or block, stucco, or vinyl.

8 **Bury propane tanks.**

If your home is served by propane, bury the tank. Do not leave it exposed. Keep barbecue grills with propane tanks far away from the exterior.

9 **Move your car.**

Park your car at least thirty feet from the home, especially if it's electric. If ignited, the car's battery may burn very hot for hours, and take your home with it.

10 Turn off gas.

If you plan to evacuate, turn off the gas before you leave.

PRO TIPS

▶ Watering your roof with a garden hose is unlikely to save your home.

▶ Do not leave sprinklers on in hopes of reducing the risk of combustion. It simply wastes water that firefighters desperately need.

▶ Double-paned windows are more heat resistant and will not crack as quickly as single-paned windows.

▶ If fire consumes any part of the home, it will likely be a total loss due to smoke damage.

HOW TO SURVIVE A TSUNAMI

1   **Observe the ocean.**

Rapidly receding or rising water is a sign that a tsunami is imminent. After an earthquake, coastal waters may recede considerably, leaving the seafloor bare.

2   **Be aware of shaking ground.**

Earthquakes and volcanic eruptions do not always cause tsunamis, but in coastal zones they should be expected. A buoy-based tsunami warning system may not be present or functioning properly. It can take from several minutes to many hours after an earthquake for a tsunami to reach land. If you feel the ground shake, be ready to take action.

3   **Listen for a roar.**

A loud, sustained roar (sometimes likened to a freight train) indicates waves moving from the deep ocean into shallow water. However, towering waves may not appear especially high from a distance, and their height may increase rapidly based on topographic characteristics of the shoreline. Bays with narrow inlets are especially vulnerable. If you can see a wave approaching, assume you cannot outrun it.

4   **Seek higher ground immediately.**

Keep going, and aim for an absolute minimum safe elevation of thirty feet above sea level. Move as far inland as possible, and remember that if you can see the wave you may be too close to escape it.

5   **Evacuate all coastlines.**

Avoid areas near bays, creeks, and rivers, as these waters may rise rapidly.

6   **Get to a high floor.**

If you are in a high-rise hotel or apartment building on the coastline and you cannot get to higher ground away from shore, move to a high floor of the building. The third floor (or higher) of a reinforced concrete structure may be a safer choice than trying to navigate a clogged evacuation route. Select a building that has its longest side perpendicular, not parallel, to the shore.

7   **Get in a car and buckle up.**

If you have no better options, get in a car, buckle the seatbelt, and keep the windows closed. The car will be swept up in the wave, but its steel frame may provide some limited, temporary protection from debris in the floodwaters. The car is likely to be carried some distance and may float until the windows are penetrated.

8   **Avoid buildings, bridges, and power lines.**

Aftershocks may occur and cause further damage, so try not to be beneath anything that could fall onto you.

PRO TIPS

- The first tsunami wave may not be the largest in a series of waves.

- Tsunamis can travel up rivers and streams that empty into the ocean.

- Flooding from a tsunami can extend inland 1,000 feet or more, covering large expanses of land with water and debris.

- The word *tsunami* means "harbor wave."

HOW TO SURVIVE A SUPERVOLCANO ERUPTION

1 **Immediately cover your mouth and nose.**

If you are caught in an ashfall event, use an N95 or equivalent mask or a respirator to prevent inhalation of ash. If no mask is available, use a shirt.

2 **Evacuate the region.**

If you are instructed to evacuate, do so. Should one erupt, supervolcanoes such as the one beneath Yellowstone National Park are likely to create vast areas of destruction, with an affected radius measured in the tens or potentially hundreds of miles.

3 **Drive, or run.**

Pyroclastic flows (a mix of hot rock, ash, pumice, and volcanic gas) move very quickly, downslope: Use a vehicle to escape. If roads are blocked or impassible, get away from lava flows, which move more slowly, on foot. Avoid valleys and natural depressions that may become filled with lava and debris as it flows away from the caldera.

4   **Avoid falling rock.**

As magma erupts explosively from the volcano, it will cool and fall back to earth as volcanic rock (pumice). If you see rocks falling, get indoors. If you are close to the volcano, falling rocks may be large and hot. To avoid being hit, turn toward their source, look up, and move out of their way as the rocks fall to earth.

5   **Protect yourself from acid rain.**

Sulfur dioxide may travel up the ash column, combine with clouds, and fall as rain laced with sulfuric acid. The acid concentration will be too low to cause burns, but vegetation can be killed and soil contaminated, creating a dead zone around the volcano that may be hundreds of square miles.

6   **Seek shelter.**

If you cannot safely evacuate, get inside. Fill a bathtub with water. Close all windows and doors, and turn off air conditioners. Use an air purifier if available. Volcanic ash is very heavy and, especially when combined with water, has the weight of cement. You roof may collapse if there is heavy ashfall.

PRO TIPS

▶   A supervolcano is a volcano with the potential to create 1,000 cubic kilometers of ejected material in a single eruption—enough to fill more than 30 billion shipping containers. This is over 1,000 times greater than the major eruption of Mount St. Helens in 1980, which killed dozens.

▸ Depending on the amount of material erupted and the height of the ash plume, a supervolcano eruption may cause global climate shifts, possibly for years, resulting in colder temperatures and crop failure.

▸ Individual explosions in an eruption sequence may occur continually or be separated by weeks, months, or even years.

▸ There have been numerous supervolcanic eruptions in Earth's history, and none have caused global extinctions. Yet.

▸ Take note of danger signs—ground movement and earthquakes, gas emissions, and more. Volcanos never erupt without warning, though some indicators may be missed if a volcano is not sufficiently monitored. Signs of an eruption may occur weeks, months, or even years before the event itself. Watch for greater-than-usual variations in ground movement, earthquakes, gas emissions, ground temperature changes, and even the formation (or draining) of lakes.

▸ Sign up for the United States Geological Survey's Volcano Notification System (https://volcanoes.usgs .gov/vns2) and follow USGSVolcanoes social media accounts for regular updates on volcanic activity in the United States.

HOW TO SURVIVE AN ASTEROID CRASH

IF THE ASTEROID IS SMALL AND CLOSE

1. **Using news reports—or the social media feeds of astronomers—determine the approximate size of the incoming asteroid.**

   Small asteroids (150 feet or less in diameter) regularly enter Earth's atmosphere with little to no warning, but you might get reports of flashes in the sky. They won't cause global damage but can be dangerous depending on their points of impact.

2. **Do not attempt to evacuate unless instructed to do so.**

   Evacuation is likely to be ordered only if the rock is spotted hours or days ahead of time, like early warnings for hurricanes and tornadoes. Small asteroids are generally not seen early, so there will probably not be sufficient time for evacuation. Shelter in place.

*Crouch under a heavy table or desk,
but avoid windows. Do not panic.*

3 **Avoid windows.**

Resist the urge to immediately run to a window to view the lightshow of the asteroid as it travels, burning, across the horizon. Even a small airburst asteroid that does not reach the ground will shatter windows and may damage hardened structures across a radius of potentially tens of miles, depending on its size and composition. To avoid being injured by flying glass, quickly get away from windows. If you are outside, get into the open, away from buildings that may collapse.

4 **Head for the basement.**
If a basement is available, move there quickly. If none is present, get to an interior room with no windows.

5 **Crouch down under a heavy table or desk.**
Get on your knees, bring your head down to your thighs, and close your eyes. Cover your ears with your hands to protect eardrums from any blast wave. Depending on the size of the airburst or impact, the location, and your distance from it, thermal radiation and seismic shock waves may be felt before you hear anything. The table or desk will likely not help in the event of a direct impact, but it will protect you if objects fall or the ceiling collapses due to vibrations. Do not venture outside until you are sure it is safe to do so.

IF THE ASTEROID IS LARGE AND FAR AWAY

1 **Do not panic.**
Larger asteroids (thousands of feet to many miles in diameter) will probably—though not definitely—be spotted by satellites well before any possible impact, potentially months or years prior. You should have time

to plan carefully before deciding to move out of the predicted impact region.

2 **Roughly determine the blast radius.**

Many factors will affect the type and extent of damage and casualties caused by a large asteroid or comet entering the atmosphere: size of the object, its composition (rock or iron, or ice for a comet), its speed and angle of entry, and where (or whether) it actually hits the Earth or just creates an airburst. For example:

▶ **A 1,000-foot dense rock asteroid**, entering the atmosphere at a (typical) 45-degree angle, traveling at average speed, that hits a landmass will cause a 4-mile-wide crater, a 3-mile fireball, a 7.0-magnitude earthquake, massive fire damage, and the collapse of buildings, bridges, and other infrastructure within **a 10-mile radius of the crater rim**.

▶ **A mile-wide iron asteroid** impacting land will destroy buildings and infrastructure within **many hundreds of miles of the impact point** but will likely not have long-term global effects.

▶ **A 5-mile-wide iron asteroid** would create an earthquake of about magnitude 10 on the Richter Scale, **greater than any earthquake in recorded history**.

▶ **A 25-mile-wide rock asteroid** impact would create a 500-mile-wide crater, have **global impacts**, and potentially kill millions. The asteroid that hit the ocean near the present-day Yucatán peninsula and most likely wiped out the dinosaurs is estimated to have been 7.5 miles wide. The extinction was caused by a combination of dust blocking the sun and killing off plant life, wildfires, tsunamis, and the depletion of the ozone layer.

3 **Do not count on evacuation.**

With sufficient warning (several years) of a medium-sized asteroid, the loss of life in the impact region might be reduced via mass evacuation. (Infrastructure, of course, would be destroyed.) However, a larger asteroid could easily wipe out a small country, making evacuation impractical, even with plenty of warning.

4 **Create a resettlement plan.**

If possible, buy property as far from the predicted impact site as possible, and plan to resettle there, with family members and belongings, well before the expected collision. Avoid coastlines, low-lying areas prone to flooding, and fault lines or areas of seismic activity. Choose property on bedrock, if available.

5 **Wait and see.**

In the most likely scenario, as the asteroid approaches, longer and more accurate observations will refine understanding of its orbital data, and the impact threat may disappear.

6 **Follow news of redirection efforts.**

If impact appears likely, authorities will attempt to redirect the trajectory of the asteroid in space (well before it threatens Earth) via impact, explosion, gravity tractor, or some combination of methods. Over time, these small nudges can alter the orbit slightly so eventually the object misses the Earth. Monitor progress and developments but be ready for failure.

7 **Resettle.**

The final weeks and months before impact will be chaotic, with mass migrations, strained resources, and closed borders. To be safe, move to your new home at least six months before the expected asteroid impact. (If it misses, you can always move back.)

8 **Be prepared for months or years of privation.**

A massive asteroid impact with global climate ramifications could interrupt the food supply. Keep emergency supplies, including seeds, on hand. See How to Prep Your Bunker, page 34, and How to Plant a Survival Garden, page 186, for details.

PRO TIPS

▸ In general, an asteroid impacting land will create a crater twenty times the rock's diameter.

▸ Comets are mostly ice, dust, rock, or metal, but typically travel at speeds two or three times greater than asteroids. They may have more destructive impacts.

▸ Research has shown that casualties from a land impact would be about an order of magnitude greater than those from a water impact, assuming identical asteroids. Because about 70 percent of the Earth's surface is covered by water, chances of a water impact are greater.

HOW TO SURVIVE THE NEXT PANDEMIC

- **Know your risk factors.**

  Jobs with close, face-to-face contact, especially those in medical and care facilities, are higher risk than those that can be performed remotely. If you cannot socially distance at work, consider a safer job or one with a flexible work schedule. If you have a high-risk job, discuss the facility's pandemic readiness strategy with management and plan accordingly.

- **Keep face masks on hand.**

  Respiratory pathogens are the most likely to spread widely. Maintain a reasonable supply of triple-layer surgical or N95 (or equivalent) masks for yourself and your family.

- **Maintain up-to-date technology.**

  You will need sufficient computer equipment (desktops or laptops, phones, web cameras) for each member of the family over preschool age—plus internet access—to perform work and school duties. If your gear is older than five years, consider replacing it.

- **Buy an air purifier.**

  Room-size air purifiers with HEPA filtration increase airflow and trap airborne contaminants, including (potentially) pathogens. Consider having at least one or two on hand, along with one set of replacement filters for each unit. Air purifiers normally cost $200 and up, but costs tend to rise sharply during pandemics and wildfire season, and supplies may be limited.

- **Store, but don't hoard.**

  Long-term disruptions in the supply of most staple consumer goods (especially food) are unlikely. Keep a thirty- to sixty-day supply of necessary, everyday, and shelf-stable items (toilet paper, canned goods, grains, soaps and detergents, shampoos) on hand to reduce trips to stores and other highly trafficked locations. Avoid storing fuels and other combustible materials unless absolutely necessary and a safe location to do so is available.

- **Design a quarantine plan.**

  Study the layout of your residence to determine appropriate areas where infected individuals can remain isolated. This may be a basement, an unused bedroom with attached bath, or a separate building like a garage apartment. The space should be well ventilated.

- **Expect shifting guidance.**

  Pathogens and their pandemics are unpredictable, and reactions should be guided by science, which may lag behind broad virus transmission. Stay flexible and ready to alter your behavior as knowledge and conditions dictate.

- **Avoid sick people.**

  Symptoms of a life-threatening virus often mimic those of other, mostly harmless viruses like those that cause the common cold: sneezing, coughing, runny nose. You'll have no way to distinguish one from the other, so assume anyone who appears sick is dangerous.

- **Avoid healthy people.**

  Respiratory viruses that are contagious during asymptomatic or presymptomatic infection are especially dangerous and likely to spread widely and rapidly. Reduce close contact with everyone outside your family unit until more data on the virus is available.

- **Avoid everyone else, especially indoor crowds.**

  Viruses spread quickly and easily in big groups of people in close contact. Indoor areas without sufficient airflow or air exchange are especially dangerous because greater viral loads can be supported. Do not enter these areas unless absolutely necessary.

- **Avoid medical and care facilities.**

  Assume everyone is infected.

- **Contact-trace.**

  Viruses spread more effectively among those who are exposed yet have no knowledge of exposure. Once you are infected or potentially infected, warn all close contacts so they can be alert for symptoms.

- **Test often.**

  Testing is an effective measure against viruses: virus testing may cause behavioral change that can reduce spread. If you are symptomatic or think you may have been exposed, get tested as soon as possible or when testing is recommended by a contact tracer.

PRO TIPS

▶ Be ready to isolate immediately.

▶ Respiratory viruses are the most transmissible among humans and are most likely to cause the next global pandemic. Reduce or eliminate contact with others to help reduce potential spread, especially in the earliest days and weeks of the new pandemic.

▶ Zoonotic respiratory viruses that jump to humans—especially those with pre- or asymptomatic spread—cannot be stopped, only mitigated using testing, protective equipment, and behavioral change.

HOW TO SURVIVE A NUCLEAR DISASTER

MELTDOWN

1 Stay calm.

Radiation danger from reactor accidents is acute in only two cases: if you are working at the facility where the meltdown is occurring—and even then, fire is likely more of an immediate danger—or if you are within the immediate radiation plume that is released.

2 Stay put.

Do not evacuate immediately unless instructed to do so. You are likely to face greater risk of injury from a traffic accident in a panicked evacuation than you are from leaking radiation.

3 Monitor wind direction.

Fasten a plastic bag to a stick and place it in the yard, visible from a window. Radiation released from an industrial accident is primarily carried by the air; it does not spread in a broad, multikilometer radius as it would from a bomb or other intentional explosion. The radioactive plume will travel with the wind. If you are upwind, you are not in danger. Even if you are downwind at the surface, winds aloft may move in other directions. If you know you will be affected by the plume, do not evacuate immediately, but be prepared to do so (See How to Pack a Go Bag in Thirty Minutes, page 24). Authorities have effective tools to detect radioactive particles and model their direction and impact.

4 **Get inside.**

Damage to structures beyond the immediate vicinity of the reactor location will be minimal to nonexistent. Close all doors and windows. Put any air conditioners on recirculate to prevent outside air from entering the building. Move to a basement, if available, or interior room as far as possible from exterior walls.

5 **Protect foods.**

Place any exposed foods (fruits and vegetables) in the refrigerator.

6 **Eat fish and salt.**

Uranium fission produces iodine 131, which is radioactive. Radioactive iodine in the plume may, in rare cases, be absorbed by the thyroid gland and cause illness, though the overall danger is probably low for most people. Saturate the thyroid with the naturally occurring safe iodine by eating fish (canned tuna is a good choice);

by consuming salty snacks; or by ingesting *small* amounts of iodized table salt (one quarter teaspoon). This will prevent radioactive iodine molecules from attaching to the thyroid gland. Consuming too much salt may raise blood pressure, which might already be high from stress. Potassium iodide (KI) pills, often taken to prevent radiation absorption in the thyroid, may cause a severe allergic reaction.

7   **Wait for instructions.**

Listen to the radio or monitor the web for instructions. Prepare to leave, but do not move until you are told where to go and how to get there. An unplanned evacuation may take you from relative safety directly into the radioactive plume.

EXPLOSION

1   **Do not panic.**

Just because an explosion or mushroom cloud is audible or visible does not mean you are in imminent danger. At night, the explosion might be visible for tens or potentially dozens of miles but may have no destructive or radiological impact at your location.

2   **Assess blast impact.**

An improvised bomb or tactical, ground-based nuclear weapon with a ten-kiloton yield will cause total destruction from explosive force and fires up to a radius of approximately one-half to one mile. Up to about four miles, most glass will be shattered, some buildings damaged, and there are likely to be countless traffic accidents. Flash blindness may also occur, especially at night, causing accidents and panic. Beyond these distances, danger from radiation will be moderate to low, and short-lived.

3   Do not attempt to travel long distances.

If affected, do not immediately attempt a full evacuation from the area. Roads may be impassible and/or infrastructure destroyed. Any attempt to get away from the area may bring you into a radiation plume or may result in being caught in the open when fallout hits.

4   Quickly get to safety.

Within the general radioactive fallout zone—several miles—you will have five to fifteen minutes to get to a safe location before fallout (essentially, radioactive sand) returns to ground level from the mushroom cloud. Follow the trinity of radiation protection: time, distance, and shielding. Grab your go bag and move fast to the nearest large building (preferably with a basement, thick walls, or both) where you can shelter.

5   Seek shelter based on your emergency plan.

All family members, regardless of location, should have identified the closest, largest building in their general vicinity beforehand, and should get there quickly. Move

After a meltdown or explosion, roads are likely to be jammed with panicked drivers—evacuate only when told to do so.

to the basement if available. Older, solid structures of stone and masonry construction offer more protection than newer buildings. To limit radiation exposure, follow the 30-30 rule: move thirty feet (three stories) underground and thirty feet from all exterior walls. If possible, identify buildings with FALLOUT SHELTER signs and pin their locations on mapping apps such as Google or Apple Maps. Help others who may need assistance get to safety.

6 **Do not venture out.**

For the first seven hours after detonation, fallout will be intensely radioactive and dangerous (See How to Deal with Fallout, page 122). Listen to the radio or monitor the web for news and instructions. Within one day, radioactive particles will have decayed significantly, and after several days it will be safe to go outside, with only a risk of moderate radiation sickness.

PRO TIPS

▸ While explosions are much more physically destructive than reactor accidents, in general their radiation danger levels are more short-lived because most of their radioactive particles decay faster. Their primary impact is the destructive force of the nuclear blast.

▸ A covert radiological attack—radiation intentionally released over time in a contained area with lots of pedestrians, such as a transit hub or shopping mall—might go undetected for long periods, and cause casualties but no physical destruction.

- A dirty bomb, where a conventional explosive is used to spread radioactive material, is not the same as a nuclear attack. Such a bomb may sow fear and panic but its destructive power and long-term health dangers are likely low.

- Staying indoors immediately after the blast is critically important because inhaled radioactive particles such as strontium, radium, and plutonium are absorbed by bones and will remain there for life.

- Sheltering in the subway may be riskier than a deep basement: blast waves may disable water pumping equipment, causing tunnels to flood. If you must shelter in the subway, stay close to a stairwell and be ready to move to higher ground at the first sign of inundation.

- Tiny homes, mobile homes, and the like provide no protection from radioactive fallout.

HOW TO DEAL WITH FALLOUT

1   **Assess bomb type.**

Significant fallout is a danger from ground-detonated nuclear weapons, not those detonated aboveground (airburst munitions). If you are outside the radius of initial destruction from an airburst bomb, you may not be in imminent danger.

2   **Remain calm.**

The danger of radioactive fallout from a ground-based nuclear detonation decreases with distance from ground zero. Except with a particularly high-yield weapon, unless you are within a mile of the blast, you are unlikely to be in imminent danger from the blast. However, the fallout plume can be dangerous up to several miles downwind for those outside.

3   **Monitor wind direction.**

Fallout is dispersed by prevailing winds. If you are within ten miles and downwind of the blast site, consider moving laterally—quickly—but only if it is safe to do so. To determine prevailing wind direction, tear a tissue into small strips and toss above you, noting direction.

4 **Find shelter.**

If you are inside, stay there. If you are outside, quickly survey surrounding buildings. Locate the largest, sturdiest nearby structure, preferably one made of stone, brick, or concrete. Keep doors and windows closed. Avoid wood-framed buildings.

5 **Move to the basement.**

If no basement is available, move to the center of the structure, as far as possible from the building's sides and roof.

6 **Monitor radiation levels.**

Radiation has no smell or taste and is undetectable without specialized equipment. If a dosimeter is available, monitor it carefully. One hundred rads per hour may result in fatal radiation poisoning in less than a day.

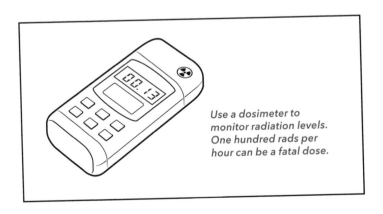

Use a dosimeter to monitor radiation levels. One hundred rads per hour can be a fatal dose.

7   **Conserve water and food.**

Take small sips and eat sparingly. If necessary, you are likely to be evacuated within a day or two, so stockpiling supplies is probably unnecessary. Water in the toilet tank can be used for drinking if needed. Do not drink from the bowl.

8   **Listen to radio for emergency instructions.**

The nature of the attack and the government response should become clear within several hours. You will be told when it is safe to go outside and, if evacuation is necessary, you'll be told the best path to follow.

PRO TIP

Radiation attenuates over time. Many radioactive particles decay following the rule of 7s: After 7 hours, radioactivity will be reduced by a factor of 10 compared to 1 hour; in 2 days the levels will have dropped by a factor of 100. After 2 weeks, it will be reduced by a factor of 1,000.

HOW TO DECONTAMINATE YOURSELF AND OTHERS

1   **Remove outer clothing as soon as practical.**

This simple action alone will remove more than 75 percent (and possibly as much as 90 percent) of radioactive contamination.

2 **Bag your clothes and place them outside your home.**

Place the garments in a large plastic bag, roll the top and tape the bag closed, then put the first bag into a second. Roll and tape. Place bagged clothing outside, in the garage, or in a disused area of your home.

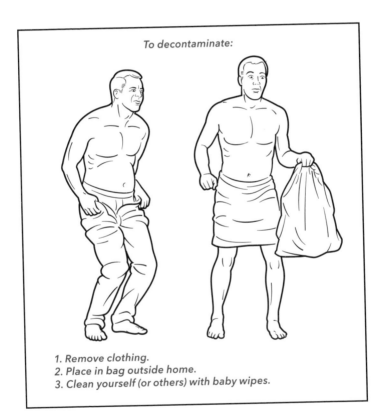

To decontaminate:

1. Remove clothing.
2. Place in bag outside home.
3. Clean yourself (or others) with baby wipes.

3 **Disinfect your body with baby wipes.**

Wiping with moist towelettes is more effective than taking a shower to remove skin contamination. When washing hair, use soap or shampoo, not conditioner, which can lock contamination into the hair.

4 **Disinfect pets.**

Wipe down or gently brush pets in a bathtub or on a plastic sheet to reduce the spread of contamination. Follow with a gentle spray of water and pet shampoo (no conditioner) and then a rinse. If practical, to reduce the spread of contamination wash the pet in an enclosed shower or behind a shower curtain in case the animal shakes itself off. Wear rubber gloves and dispose of as above.

PRO TIP

Do not shave the pet's hair or fur: this can cause nicks or cuts that may introduce contamination into the animal's bloodstream.

Brush or wipe down pets in a bathtub, and then rinse them with water.

Surviving the
Aftermath

HOW TO DETERMINE IF CONDITIONS ARE SAFE

1   **Check for noxious odors.**

While some toxins—particularly nerve agents—have no odor, many dangerous chemical liquids and gases do. If you smell bleach (chlorine), sulfur or rotten eggs or "sewer gas" (hydrogen sulfide), or cat urine (ammonia) poisonous gas may be near your location.

2   **Be alert for detonations.**

Explosions and thick black smoke are obvious danger signs but may not necessarily, or always, indicate casualties in your immediate vicinity.

3   **Monitor wind direction.**

Gases and radioactive particles travel with the wind. However, upper air currents may be different than winds at ground level. Being upwind of a hazard does not mean conditions are safe. They may deteriorate quickly.

Before going outside, look for signs that conditions are safe.
Dead wildlife, emergency vehicles, and plumes of smoke
are signs that you should stay put.

4 Look for dead wildlife.

Birds are highly sensitive to airborne toxins and will succumb quickly. If you see pigeons, sparrows, or other common birds dropping mid-flight, or dead on the ground, conditions are likely unsafe for humans. Ground mammals such as squirrels and chipmunks are also likely to be killed quickly by chemical agents. Biological agents, however, may take longer to act, and infected animals may not expire immediately. Low to moderate doses of radiation may have no immediate effects on animals or humans.

5 Check for emergency responders.

If you hear or see them, it's probably safe to emerge. The absence of moving vehicles with sirens may indicate that first responders have succumbed to an airborne toxin. Some chemical explosions may remove so much oxygen from the air that vehicles are unable to start.

PRO TIP

While a canary in a cage (the so-called bird box) can be effective for some seeping gases like carbon monoxide, if a bird you are carrying expires you probably will too.

HOW TO MAKE AN EMERGENCY AIR FILTER

1 **Obtain a square box fan.**

The larger the room, the bigger the fan should be. A standard twenty-inch fan should be sufficient for a small room. Big rooms may require more. Keep unplugged.

2 **Get a basic filter.**

The greater the filtration, the cleaner the air. At minimum, use a furnace or central air conditioning filter with a minimum efficiency reporting value (MERV) rating of 5. MERV rating indicates the filter's ability to capture airborne particles. The higher the rating, the smaller the particles the filter can capture. A filter with a rating of 16 will capture particles .3 to 1.0 microns in diameter, while one with a 6 rating may only capture particles from 3 to 10 microns.

3 **Add a HEPA filter.**

If you have only a low-MERV filter, a high efficiency particulate air (HEPA) filter should be added. This type of air filter can theoretically remove at least 99.97 percent of dust, pollen, mold, bacteria, and any airborne particles with a size of .3 microns or larger.

4   **Attach it to the back of the fan.**

Using strong duct tape, first tape the HEPA filter, if you are using one, to the back of the fan along all four edges. If the filter is too small, cut two filters to fit and tape them together, then to the fan. The entire rear surface of the fan should be covered. The HEPA filter should have an indicator of air flow direction. Make sure to tape it in the proper orientation.

5   **Add MERV.**

Tape the MERV filter to the HEPA filter along its edges, or directly to the fan if you're only using the MERV. Do not leave gaps. Cut two filters, if necessary, as described above.

6   **Turn fan on.**

Plug in the fan and turn it on high. Air will enter the rear of the fan and particles should be trapped within the filters.

7   **Check the air flow.**

Turn the fan speed down. If air still flows sufficiently through the fan at lower speeds, you can use the lower setting to reduce noise (at the expense of lower air flow and less filtration.)

8 **Clear or replace filters regularly.**

Depending on particulate matter in the air, the filters may become dirty or clogged rapidly, reducing their efficiency. HEPA filters should be discarded and replaced once they turn gray or black. Some brands of MERV filter (especially those with metal mesh) may be reused: vacuum it, then wash it with warm soapy water and allow it to dry completely. Eventually the filter will begin to disintegrate and should be replaced.

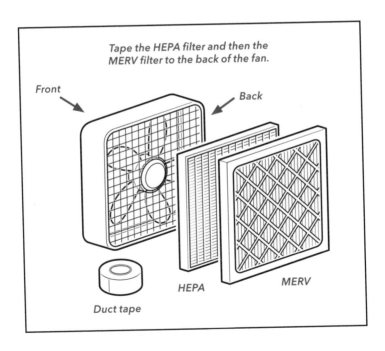

Tape the HEPA filter and then the MERV filter to the back of the fan.

Front

Back

Duct tape

HEPA

MERV

HOW TO MAKE AN EMERGENCY GAS MASK

A powered air purifier or blower–based protection system is easy to construct and does not require a tight seal around the face, which can be difficult to achieve, uncomfortable, and may hinder mobility. Instead, this system uses a fan to blow filtered air over the head, reducing contaminants that may be inhaled.

1 **Obtain a blower fan.**

Find a centrifugal fan or blower, like the type used for computers, that can be powered by batteries. Good airflow output is essential: two fans are better than one.

2 **Add tubing.**

Get a four-foot length of nonporous plastic or rubber tubing, three-quarters to one inch in diameter. Surgical tubing is best, but a garden hose will work. Cut a one-foot section (or shorter, if feasible). Using duct tape, attach this to the outlet of the blower. If necessary, use a funnel between them: wide end at the fan, narrow end taped to the hose. Less hose will result in better airflow.

3 **Prepare the filter.**

Find a metal coffee can or other tin with a screw top lid. Cut or punch a one-inch hole in the bottom of the can. Remove the screw top. If available, place a small section of metal mesh or thick window screen in the bottom of the can to cover the opening, for retaining carbon. Cut a disc of furnace filter and place over the screen, to prevent small particles from falling out, and to catch dust.

4 **Fill the can with charcoal.**

Begin to fill the can with activated carbon (charcoal), widely available online; use activated charcoal from an aquarium filter as a last resort. Do not use barbecue charcoal or charred wood chips. Pack the carbon as densely as possible: add it slowly, then shake the can to settle and compress. Repeat. Once the can is full, compact the contents even further by tamping it down using a full can of soda, a large spoon, or another implement that fits in the can. Add a second filter pad on top of the carbon bed, and then a layer of screen or mesh.

5 **Attach funnel and filter.**

Using a funnel with a narrow end that can fit the hose, and a wide end that can fit the filter can, tape the hose running from the blower to the narrow end. Get a cup-shaped N95 face mask and press the narrow end into the funnel. Tape the wide end of the funnel and its N95 filter to the bottom of the can.

6   **Affix tubing to top.**

Cut a hole in the screw top, insert one end of the longer section of tubing, and secure it with tape. Screw lid onto the filter (the can). Seal any gaps with tape.

7   **Test the fan.**

Turn the fan on high. Air will be pulled into the fan, travel through the first section of tube and through the N95 filter, and be cleaned by the activated carbon. It will then travel out of the can and down the longer section of tubing. You should feel the air flow out of the tube. If you don't, check for leaks. You may need to add a more powerful blower if the flow is not high enough.

8   **Make a hood.**

Find a thick plastic bag (a turkey roasting bag works well), large enough to cover your head and reach your shoulders. Using scissors, cut away a section of the bag where your face will be. With the duct tape, secure a piece of clear plastic, such as from a three-liter soda bottle, over the hole. This will allow you to see. You must create a good seal between the plastic and the bag, with no gaps.

9   **Attach the hose.**

Cut a small hole in the bag level with the top of the neck on the side opposite the eyepiece, insert the free end of tubing, and tape to seal. Affix the fan and filter to a holder on your belt or carry them.

10 Test the airflow.

With the system complete, run the blower. Place the bag on a table, smooth it flat, and then close the open end as tightly as possible. Check that the bag inflates to the maximum within three seconds. If not, additional blower capacity is needed.

11 Place the bag on your head and secure the bag around your neck.

Position the bag so you can see through the plastic window. Using string or elastic bands, gather the bag loosely around your neck. You are not making an airtight seal: the bag should be retained enough to stay in place, but not so tight against your neck that no air can flow out of the hood.

12 Test once more.

Turn the fan on. Dirty air will be pulled into the fan, travel to the filter, be cleaned, and then flow into the hood from the tube and out from the neck opening.

PRO TIPS

▶ If the fan fails, the hood will not protect you and should be removed immediately.

▶ Plain activated carbon offers protection against organic vapors, but not all toxic agents, gases, biological weapons, or radioactive fallout.

▶ If time allows, purchase a mask with multigas cartridges with integral P-100 filtration.

- Respirators without eye protection don't protect the eyes from irritating or toxic gases or particles.

- Filters don't make oxygen, they only clean the air.

HOW TO SURVIVE TEAR GAS

1 **Survey surroundings quickly.**

When tear gas is released, it mixes into the air and fills up available space with a toxic cloud. If you suspect tear gas may be deployed, memorize as much of your surroundings as possible, including the locations of nearby exit routes like open streets and fixed obstacles including parked cars, streetlights, and crowd-control barriers. This will make navigation and escape easier after you've been temporarily blinded by the gas.

2 **Stay calm.**

While you may be temporarily blinded, serious or permanent injury from the gas is unlikely. You are more likely to be injured by dangerous collisions with panicked protesters, fixed obstacles, or authorities.

3 **Protect your face and airway.**

Immediately close your eyes and cover your nose and eyes with your shirt, a cloth hat, a bag, or your hands. (Wear a handkerchief or scarf for this purpose. Soaking the cloth in lemon juice or Coca-Cola prior to use may reduce the pain of tear gas exposure.)

4   **Move fast.**

Locate the nearest exit route or open area that has not been hit. Gas travels downwind, so avoid running with the wind. Run upwind or laterally to escape clouds of gas, moving to a higher elevation if possible. Tear gas can linger in the air for hours or in rare cases days: do not assume you are safe just because some time has passed.

5   **Keep your eyes closed.**

Resist the temptation to open your eyes until you have clear, cool water available to rinse them. Once away from the gas, move protective clothing (or hands) away from your face to reduce continued exposure to any gas that may have collected on them.

6   **Rinse.**

Rinse your eyes and airway with clean water to clear the chemical from your face. After exposure, get rid of or wash any clothing that has been in contact with tear gas.

PRO TIPS

▶   Despite its name, tear gas is not a true gas. The chemicals are solids and typically dispersed within a thick fog. The chemicals trigger tears, but even exposure to small amounts of tear gas can cause other discomfort: burning eyes, pain in your nose, nausea, chest tightness, shortness of breath, stomachache, and diarrhea.

▶ A solution of liquid antacid—mixed 50-50 with water—sprayed into the eyes and mouth (and swallowed) may reduce the effects of tear gas.

HOW TO LOCATE OTHER OPPORTUNISTIC TOOLS (LOOT)

1 Determine the nature of your (or your group's) needs:

- ▶ Food

- ▶ Shelter

- ▶ Medicine/Supplies

- ▶ Safety

- ▶ Tools

2 Obtain a vehicle.

This may not always be possible, but using a vehicle is ideal for maximum efficiency.

3 Decide if you should focus first on security or utility.

This will likely depend on the amount of postdisaster chaos.

4 **If chaos is abundant, head to your local sporting goods store or gun store.**

Select a shotgun or rifle if possible, as well as ammunition and knives.

5 **Head to a hardware store for essential tools and supplies.**

Focus on items that may help provide power, construct permanent shelters or barriers, provide protection from fallout or pollution (such as air filters or gas masks, or hazmat suits), or items that can provide both utility and protection (such as chainsaws).

6 **Go to a drugstore for medical and hygiene supplies.**

7 **The grocery store should be your last stop—most noncanned foods will be inedible and it will be best to hunt for and gather your meals.**

HOW TO MAKE HUNTING TOOLS

RABBIT STICK

1 **Cut wood for the stick.**

With an axe or knife, cut a length of hard wood about as long as your forearm and 1½ inches in diameter. It need not be perfectly straight.

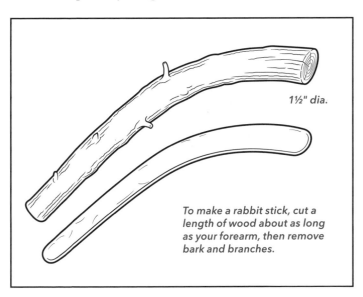

1½" dia.

To make a rabbit stick, cut a length of wood about as long as your forearm, then remove bark and branches.

2   Remove the bark and any branches.

3   Practice throwing it.

A rabbit stick is good for hitting a small target up to ten feet away. Use it to stun or kill rabbits, beavers, birds, and other small forest dwellers.

ATLATL (OR SPEAR THROWER)

1   Fashion or find a suitable piece of wood for the atlatl.

You need a flat piece of wood about 12 inches long, 1½ inches wide, and ½ inch thick.

2   Carve the wood.

Carve one end to fit your hand; this will be the handle. On the other end, carve a notch or divot which the back of the spear will rest in.

3   Make the spear.

Find a branch about 6 to 8 feet long and ½ inch in diameter. It need not be perfectly straight. Clean off bark and branches. Round off the throwing end, then sharpen the killing end and harden it by roasting in a fire until blackened. Alternatively, grind a piece of bone or stone to a point, then tie it tightly onto the end of the spear.

4 **Throw the spear using the atlatl.**

Hold the atlatl over one shoulder, with the handle in your hand and the divot end pointing behind you. Rest the spear along it, with the back end of the spear sitting in the notch. Whip the handle forward and down to launch the spear away from you at high velocity.

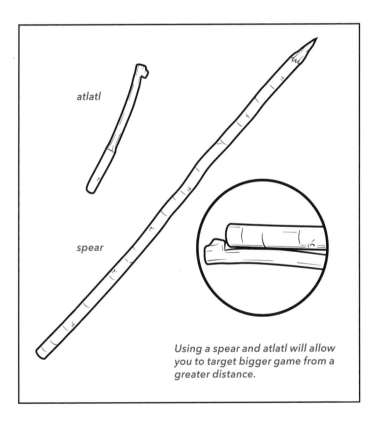

atlatl

spear

Using a spear and atlatl will allow you to target bigger game from a greater distance.

WOOMERA (OR THROWING ARROW)

The Australian woomera has a slightly different design than the atlatl, doubles as a digging stick, and is used to launch an arrow, not a spear.

Find a flat piece of wood about 12 inches long, several inches wide, and ½ inch thick to make into the woomera. Carve one end into a handle as above, and carve the other end into a point like a spade. As above, carve a notch or divot into the spade end. Choose a piece of wood that is ¼ to ½ inch in diameter and just a few feet long, and fashion it into an arrow. A good woomera will easily launch a short projectile 100 to 200 yards.

PRO TIP

You can treat spear and arrow tips with sap from the Canadian buffaloberry shrub (*Shepherdia canadensis*), which causes victims to go into anaphylactic shock within seconds. The berries themselves are edible, and are a food of choice for bears. Humans tend to avoid them due to their bitterness but they can be eaten safely, as long as the sap is avoided.

HOW TO REMOVE A SPEAR OR ARROW FROM YOUR LEG

1 **Control the bleeding.**

Regardless of whether the spear has passed through you or is embedded, control the bleeding as soon as possible. Apply immediate, steady pressure to the wound area using a folded shirt, thick sock, or other piece of clothing, the cleaner the better. Blood that is seeping but not spurting indicates the arrow likely missed an artery, so you may have some time to seek help. Once the bleeding has slowed or stopped, tear strips of fabric and wrap the strips across the cloth, around your leg, and then tie off. The strips should be tight. If available, get medical assistance.

2 **Make a tourniquet.**

If the arrow has injured an artery, or professional medical treatment is too far away or no longer available, removal of the arrow in the field will be your only option. You will need a tourniquet (a leather belt or two-inch-wide strip of cloth) and a windlass (stout rod or stick, to tighten tourniquet).

3 **Position the tourniquet.**

Loosely wrap the tourniquet around your leg above the arrow entry point. Tie off, leaving a foot of loose ends.

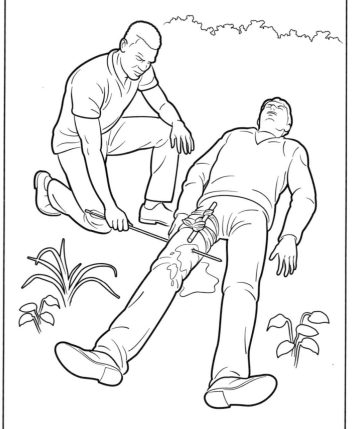

To remove an arrow that has gone all the way through the body:

1. Tie a tourniquet above the wound.
2. Tighten using a windlass.
3. Remove the arrowhead, then pull the arrow out.

4 Place the windlass over tourniquet and tie the loose ends in a knot over the windlass.

Turn the windlass until it is extremely tight.

5 Test if the tourniquet is tight enough.

Press the area around the wound. If there is no capillary refill (the pressed area remains white), it is sufficiently tight. Otherwise, tighten further.

6 Tie another knot over the windlass to secure it.

7 Probe the wound to see if the arrowhead is embedded.

If the arrow is embedded, do not attempt to push it through tissue, which may further damage nerves or blood vessels in front of the arrowhead. Probe the wound with a boiled (sterilized) tool or a clean finger to see if it is embedded in bone. Arrows embedded in bone will require considerably more force to remove.

8 Remove the arrowhead if it has punctured the leg through an exit wound.

If the arrowhead has punctured the skin through an exit wound, cut off the arrowhead with a bush knife or axe before removal of the shaft.

9 If the arrowhead is still embedded, grip the arrow as close to skin as possible and pull outwards.

Pull the arrow out by matching its entry direction and angle. There will likely be more bleeding once the arrow is removed, so be ready to apply direct pressure or a tourniquet (see above).

10 Clean and wrap the wound.

PRO TIPS

▶   Whenever possible, leave the arrow in place until you can reach medical care, or at least a location that is warm, clean, and has good light.

▶   A tourniquet may be safely left in place for up to about six hours before downstream tissue is permanently damaged from lack of blood supply.

HOW TO SKIN ANIMALS AND TAN HIDES

Small, fur-covered animals like rabbits and beavers are relatively easy to catch and kill, and their skins can be tanned to make rawhide or leather, which is long-lasting and has multiple uses. Larger game such as deer, elk, and moose will be more challenging and time-consuming, but produce more leather.

RAWHIDE

1 **Disembowel the animal.**

Using your knife, cut open the animal's belly from neck to anus and remove the entrails and organs. Cut off the head and set it aside: you will need it later.

2 **Hang the animal by its hind legs, then peel and cut off the skin.**

Working deliberately, peel by tugging at the skin rather than using your knife too much, which can damage the hide. Use your fingers or fist to push the hide from the carcass, using your knife only to cut through any membrane when necessary.

3   **Scrape the fat off the inside of the hide.**

Place the hide, inside out, on a flat log at waist height and scrape the fat off using your knife or a sharpened bone.

4   **Remove the fur.**

Flip the pelt over and carefully scrape the fur off, going against its natural direction of growth. It may take a while, so be patient. If it's a soft fur from a rabbit or fox, you may choose to leave it on for added comfort as clothing.

5   **Dry the hide for a day.**

After both sides have been thoroughly scraped, allow the hide to dry for at least twenty-four hours (longer in damp weather). If it's raining, dry the hide under shelter.

6   **Cut into strips to make rope, or fold or cut into panels and sew together to make other useful items.**

TANNED HIDE

1   **Follow the above instructions for rawhide.**

2   **Make a brain slurry.**

Crack the skull of the animal with your knife or bush axe and remove its brain. Chop the brain into small pieces, place the pieces in a pot, and mix them with warm water to make a thick slurry. (For small animals, you may need more than one brain.)

3 **Soak the hide.**

Soak the animal hide in the slurry for about twenty minutes to help it absorb the oils from the brain. This step will help soften the hide.

4 **Let it dry.**

5 Wring the hide around a stick to remove all moisture, then stretch it by hand. (To preserve a hide with fur, rub the brain mix into the inside of the hide until it is absorbed by the dry skin.)

6 **Smoke the hide to set the tan.**

Stretch the hide between two sticks, grain-side (the side that used to have fur) down, a few feet off the ground. Try to form the hide into a cone that will capture the smoke inside. At night only, build a fire below. The smoke will help set the tan, changing the chemistry of the fibers and helping to keep the hide soft if it gets wet. Smoke it for several hours.

7 Once tanned, hides can be used for clothing, bags, and as waterproofing for the top of a pit shelter.

HOW TO EAT INSECTS AND RODENTS

INSECTS

1 **Identify insects that are safe to eat by their color.**

With a few exceptions, most dull-colored insects—brown, black, or white (grubs)—found in the US are safe to eat, once cooked. Brightly colored insects (butterflies, ladybugs, and green, red, or yellow grasshoppers), millipedes, and hairy caterpillars should be avoided.

2 **Determine your nutritional requirements.**

An average-size adult requires around 60 grams of protein per day. Insects are mostly water and exoskeleton. You will need to eat a *lot* of them if they will be your primary protein source. Cooking reduces weight by about 75 percent, and 40 to 70 percent of what remains will be protein. Consider choosing grubs and larvae, which have no exoskeletons, are higher in protein, and are easy to forage (below).

Cooking insects and grubs before eating will remove bacteria and add to deliciousness.

3 **Catch or forage your meal.**

In cold climates and in the winter months, finding insects may be difficult. In these conditions, turn over rotted logs and other decomposing vegetation and dig for grubs. If available, leave fruit or vegetables out to rot. They will attract insects—and produce grubs or larvae—within a few days unless it's very cold.

4 **Remove stingers, and legs and wings (optional).**
Stingers from bees and stinging insects should be removed. Wings and legs may be removed to make the bugs more palatable (and reduce the chance of choking) if you intend to eat them whole.

5 **Cook the insects to eliminate bacteria.**
Without exception, cook all insects before eating to eliminate bacteria and pathogens that may be on their bodies. (There have been no documented reports of zoonotic transmission from cooked insects to humans.) Boil for five to ten minutes, then roast them over a fire in a pot or bowl or on a metal tray, or on a stick. Once cooked, the bugs may be crushed between two rocks and the powder added to liquid or sprinkled on other foods to make them more appetizing.

PRO TIPS

▸ Good insect meal choices include grubs, locusts and brown grasshoppers, honeybees (with stingers removed), beetles (limited protein value but easy to catch), cicadas, ants, termites, and cockroaches.

▸ Eat a small amount of any insect before you gorge on a huge meal of them.

▸ Insects have chitin (fibrous material) in their exoskeletons and consuming them may be dangerous for those allergic to crustaceans (shrimp, crab, lobster, and so on).

▸ While not insects, earthworms can also be eaten.

RODENTS AND SMALL MAMMALS

1 **Determine where the rodent lives and its diet.**

Most wild rodents are safe to eat when properly prepared. Urban rodents such as sewer rats often carry disease and should be avoided. Chipmunks, squirrels, prairie dogs, rabbits, and other small rodents or ground mammals that subsist on nuts, seeds, grasses, and insects are good choices.

2 **Kill the animal and remove its fur.**

Once caught in a trap, small wild rodents can be drowned quickly in a bucket. Remove fur, and note that ticks and mites may be present. (See How to Skin Animals and Tan Hides, page 153.)

3 **Remove its head, tail, and entrails.**

Use a hunting knife to gut the animal and clean it. If you leave the head on, avoid eating the brain of the animal.

4 **Roast the animal on a stake or spit over a fire until the meat is thoroughly cooked.**

HOW TO FORAGE

In winter, insects, mushrooms, and edible berries and flowers may be in short supply. If the ground is frozen, you will need a shovel and a small axe to break up and move dead wood in search of grubs. Decomposing plant and animal matter creates heat, which will attract insects.

WOODLANDS

- **Look for rotting wood.**

  Decomposing wood may hide termites and their grubs underneath. Collect then cook them before eating. Grasshoppers and beetles may also be present.

- **Look for mushrooms.**

  Differentiating edible from poisonous mushrooms can be very difficult without a knowledgeable guidebook (or guide). However, mushrooms are a good indication of nutrients in the soil. Carefully move rotting vegetation around the fungus and look for beetles and grubs. Collect the insects and cook them.

- **Look for dung and rotting animal carcasses.**

  Both are good sources of grubs, which should be cleaned (preferably by boiling) before roasting and eating.

- **Stake out flowers and watch for bees.**

  Flowers will attract bees. Follow the bees back to their hive to access the honey; wear protective clothing and/or smoke the hive to slow the bees down and reduce the chances of being stung. The bees themselves can also be cooked and eaten after removing their stingers.

- **Look for fruit trees.**

  Ripe fruit and berries can be eaten off trees and bushes. Don't ignore the rotting fruit on the ground: it will attract bees that become drunk on the fermenting sugars, making them easy to swat to the ground and kill.

GRASSLANDS

- **Check mounds.**

  Large earthen mounds may contain ants or termites. They (and their grubs) can be cooked and eaten. Avoid red fire ants which have a painful bite and will attack any disturbance to the mound that covers their nest.

- **Collect spiders and crickets.**

  Avoid crickets that are caught in spiderwebs, which will probably have been poisoned.

- **Check under fallen trees.**

  These may cover insects, as above, but may also be hiding snakes, especially juveniles that feed on bugs. Use caution.

DESERT

- **Use sounds to locate edible insects.**

  Crickets, locusts, cicadas, dragonflies, and other flying insects can be tracked by the sounds they make, especially in the early evening or morning hours. Amphibians that eat them (especially frogs) can similarly be tracked, caught, cooked, and eaten.

- **Forage at night.**

  Insects will be more mobile and easier to spot and catch during cooler nighttime hours. Use a flashlight or lantern to attract them. Watering holes or other damp areas will naturally attract insects.

- **Check under rocks.**

  Desert arthropods (centipedes, scorpions) often hide and burrow under rocks. Use caution or you risk a painful, venomous bite or sting. Arthropods are mostly exoskeleton and their protein value is low, so these should not be your first meal choice.

- **Wait for rain.**

  Areas that naturally collect water (depressions, gullies, dry washes) will be teeming with insect life after a hard rain.

EDIBLE AND MEDICINAL PLANTS

- **Common dandelion (*Taraxacum officinale*)**

  Dandelions are found on all continents save Antarctica. All parts of the plant itself (flowers, leaves, and stems) are edible, can be eaten raw or cooked, and contain lots of vitamins and minerals, and some protein and fat. Roots must be cooked: clean them before adding to soups or stews. In a pinch, thinly slice the roots, dry roast in a pan over a fire until dark brown, then crush. Add water and boil the mixture to make ersatz coffee.

  Dandelion roots contain inulin, a prebiotic carbohydrate and soluble fiber that aids the growth of healthy bacteria in the digestive system and supports calcium absorption. They help to slow digestion, but also contain a mild laxative to help relieve constipation.

- **Common yarrow (*Achillea millefolium*)**

  There are several species of yarrow, and all have high levels of vitamins, including vitamins B_1 and C, as well as some protein. Cut up the leaves and sprinkle on food or boil the leaves and flowers to make infusions (tea) to relieve diarrhea and stomach cramps.

  When poured over cuts, scrapes, and rashes, the infusions have antibiotic properties and will accelerate healing. Chew the leaves or roots to help treat mouth infections and rub the leaves and their sap on exposed skin to deter mosquitoes.

- **Pine tree (*Pinaceae*)**

There are dozens of species of pine tree, and most are safe to consume, as below. The loblolly pine (*Pinus taede*) should be avoided, and another, *Pinus californiarum*, also known as the single-leaf pinyon-pine, has nuts that are edible, but the rest of the tree should be avoided.

Chew raw pine needles to extract the nutrients—including small amounts of protein and fat—or brew them to make tea. The needles are high in vitamins A and C, and indigenous peoples often ate them to prevent scurvy. The needles also contain minerals including calcium, iron, phosphorous, and manganese. The sap from the tree can be chewed to relieve a sore throat, but avoid swallowing it.

The small nuts on pinecones (called, appropriately enough, pine nuts) are edible, and are highly nutritious and filled with protein and vitamins. Even better, in the spring, male pinecones will be covered in pollen. Snap them off the tree, place in a bag, and shake the cones to release their pollen. The pollen is nutritious and includes vitamins A, B_1, B_2, B_3, B_6, B_9, C, E, and D.

- **Plantain (*Plantago major*)**

  Not to be confused with the banana-like fruit of the same name, the plantain (also called white man's footprint, owing to its appearance shortly after European colonizers arrived) is common in many parts of the US and Europe. Eat the leaves, which are filled with vitamins and have a bitter taste, raw or cooked. Remove the seeds, which are high in vitamin B_1, allow to soak overnight, then eat. They will have a gruel-like consistency and are high in carbohydrates, and are also bitter. Grind the seeds to make a flour substitute.

    Mash the leaves and use as a plaster or poultice to help small infected wounds heal faster. Chew a leaf into a pulp and place on insect stings for an hour to relieve pain. Teas and infusions made from the leaves will help relieve diarrhea.

HOW TO DETERMINE WHO TO EAT FIRST

- **Eat the first person who passes away.**

  Their meat will remain edible for twenty-four hours, depending on the elements.

- **Choose a stranger or an evil person.**

  Psychological and emotional attachments will make consuming family members quite difficult; even former spouses will be a challenge in most cases. Acrimonious divorces might make cannibalizing your former partner appear attractive at first, but remember: this might be the parent of your children.

  You may feel better (if not good) consuming an individual the collective group views as bad, mean, evil, or terroristic. So-called aggressive cannibalistic societies have been known to use this method in selecting victims. However, a recent personal insult or habit you find irritating should not be grounds to threaten someone with consumption.

- **Select the person based on nutritional needs.**
  A family of four will require many more calories than a single person. Cannibalizing a person of very small stature may leave your group hungry, while a larger individual may provide more adequate sustenance.

- **Select the person based on their utility and skills.**
  Do not consume someone who is essential for surviving the situation (for example, the only person who can pilot an escape vehicle or who knows how to build fires). Diseased or emaciated individuals should be avoided except as a last resort.

PRO TIPS

- ▸ Avoid consuming human brains, which may carry prions (misfolded proteins) that can infect healthy cells and lead to kuru, a fatal neurodegenerative disease.

- ▸ While ritualistic drinking of blood was common among some societies in the past, consuming it may lead to iron toxicity, which can cause spasms, confusion, and possibly death.

- ▸ Meals should be roasted or boiled. Crack bones before boiling to release marrow, which is high in nutrients. Raw flesh should be avoided: it is very tough and will be difficult to chew and digest, and may carry disease.

HOW TO DRINK YOUR OWN URINE

While urine is mostly free of pathogens, drinking large quantities in a short period of time may lead to kidney failure. Take the following steps to make your pee safer to drink.

1 **Obtain a glass jar or other container.**

Urine contains dissolved minerals—salt, potassium, phosphorus—and chemicals (primarily urea and uric acid) that can make you sick: do not drink warm urine. Urinate into a container and set it aside.

2 **Wait several days.**

Leave the container at room temperature for three days if time allows. Over time, naturally occurring urease enzymes will decompose the urea (the major constituent in urine, aside from water), forming ammonia and ammonium ion. This process will make the urine smell terrible but will make it easier to treat chemically.

3 **Add a handful of ash.**

Ash, as from a wood fire, adds alkali to the urine and will raise the pH (alkalinity). This process will convert most of the ammonium ion to ammonia. While ammonia is quite

Boiling filtered urine for a few minutes will cook off ammonia and pathogens and make it safe to consume.

volatile, it's easy to remove. Allow the mixture to sit for several hours, then strain if possible.

4 **Boil the urine for a few minutes.**

This will cook off the ammonia (as well as any remaining pathogens) and make the urine safe to consume. Allow it to cool before enjoying.

PRO TIPS

▶ Urine is the result of your kidneys removing compounds your body cannot store. Do not drink regularly.

▶ As you become more dehydrated, your kidneys will stop making urine.

► Assuming it is free of pathogens—and you won't know one way or the other—drinking small amounts of blood (up to 100ml/day) is unlikely to hurt you. Small quantities of animal blood, such as found in raw or rare meats, is usually diluted and (mostly) safe, unless there is a pathogen such as E. coli present. However, blood is relatively high in sodium and drinking it in quantity will result in dehydration, as well as iron toxicity and possible death. (See How to Determine Who to Eat First, page 166.)

DIRTY WATER

You can purify water from unknown origins (with some exceptions; see Fresh Water, below) using filtration.

1 Make charcoal.

Build a very hot fire and burn large pieces of wood until what remains is completely black. Remove ash. You will be left with charred coals. Allow them to cool.

2 Break the charcoal into small pieces.

3 Activate the charcoal.

Dissolve 250 grams of calcium chloride in 1,000 ml of water. Calcium chloride, an inorganic salt, is available in home brewing, specialty food, and drug stores, and is often sold as ice melter in hardware stores. Mix the charcoal with the solution and allow to dry. You have now activated the charcoal, making it highly absorptive.

4 Build pipe purifier.

Using a pipe or other hollow cylinder, place fabric—a shirt works well—over one end and secure it. Pack the vessel with the charcoal. Cover the other end with more fabric. If no pipe is available, cover the top of a bowl or can with the shirt, secure it, and dump the charcoal on top.

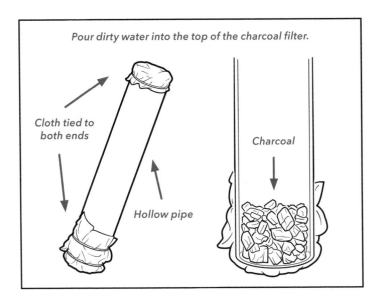

Pour dirty water into the top of the charcoal filter.

Cloth tied to both ends

Charcoal

Hollow pipe

5 Place a bowl or other container at the bottom of the pipe and pour the water into the pipe through the top.

Hold the pipe vertically. Very slowly pour the water through the fabric on top.

Place a container under the bottom to catch the water as it filters through the charcoal. The filtration process will remove trace chemicals and make the water safer to drink.

6 **Boil the filtered water if possible, to remove any microbial contaminants.**

Boil for five minutes and then allow to cool before drinking.

PRO TIP

Sunlight and its ultraviolet radiation can be used to provide some purification, especially if direct light heats the water. Place the water in a clear bottle, open pan, or shallow container and expose to direct sunlight over several days. Use this method only if you cannot build a fire.

SEA WATER

Without desalinization, drinking sea water will lead to dehydration, kidney failure, and likely death. Build a solar still to desalinate the water and make it drinkable via evaporation.

1 **Dig a pit.**

Dig a shallow pit in the ground, about one foot deep and a few feet in diameter. The hole should be exposed to the sun for as much of the day as possible.

2   **Line the pit with a tarp.**

Line the cavity with a tarp or other nonporous material to prevent the sea water from being absorbed into the soil or sand.

3   **Place a tall bottle, can, or another similar receptacle in the center of the pit.**

The top should be an inch or two below the top of the hole.

4   **Fill the hole with sea water.**

5   **Cover the hole completely with another tarp or other plastic.**

The clearer the plastic you can use, the better. Place rocks on the cover around the edges of the hole to keep it in place. It should not be too taut.

6   **Place a stone or rock at the center of the tarp directly above the can.**

The rock should weigh the tarp down slightly so that there is an indentation.

7   **Wait for a day or more.**

As solar radiation heats the sea water, it will evaporate. Condensation will form on the inside of the tarp and flow down to the center point below the rock, where it will slowly drip into the can. This water, with the salt left behind, is now safe to drink. Repeat with additional sea water, scooping out any salt residue as needed.

PRO TIP

Boiling sea water does not make it potable. However, boiling will create steam and condensation, which can be captured and consumed.

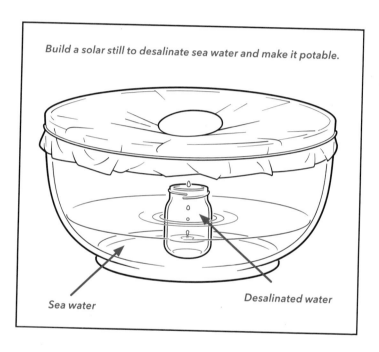

Build a solar still to desalinate sea water and make it potable.

Sea water

Desalinated water

FRESH WATER

Rainwater is generally safe to drink, provided it does not sit and stagnate. Use the following as a guide to determine if other water sources are safe for consumption.

- **Determine elevation of water source.**

  Generally, the higher the elevation of the source of the water, the safer it is. Avoid water that is below (or downstream of) farms with livestock: it may be polluted with agricultural, microbial, or bacterial contaminants. Meltwater from recent snow is generally safe to drink.

- **Check flow.**

  The more oxygenated the water source, the safer it is likely to be. Shallow, fast-flowing streams and creeks—with the exceptions noted above—are generally safer sources of drinking water than meandering rivers, creeks, or lakes.

- **Smell and check color.**

  The water should not smell odd or off, or have a greenish tint. Both can indicate the presence of algae, which may be associated with cyanobacteria, which can be toxic.

- **Check fish.**

  The presence of live fish in a body of water does not indicate the water is safe for consumption. However, water with lots of dead fish should be avoided.

- **Purify water from unknown sources when possible.**

  If you are not certain the water is safe to drink, you should purify it before drinking (see Dirty Water above) unless you are severely dehydrated.

Industrial and chemical plants are often located on streams, creeks, and rivers. Be wary of consuming water downstream of these facilities.

RAW FOODS

Many raw fruits and vegetables—not just watermelon—are 80 to 90 percent water, making them good choices for rehydration. Most can be eaten unprepared, but they can also be smashed or chopped and the liquid removed via straining or squeezing.

▶ Celery and cucumber: More than 90 percent water

▶ Zucchini: About 90 percent water

▶ Watercress: Grows on water, is mostly water

▶ Apples: High in water, plus vitamins

▶ Lettuce: Mostly water, especially iceberg

▶ Tomatoes: Lots of water (one cup of raw tomato contains more than 150 grams of water)

▶ Mangoes and blueberries: Around 80 percent water, depending on variety

▶ Pineapple, strawberries, oranges: Plenty of water, plus vitamins

PRO TIP

Dehydrated fruits and vegetables will not keep you hydrated.

HOW TO BUILD SHELTER IN AN EXTREME CLIMATE

FROZEN

In a frozen climate, a quinzhee (snow cave) will provide you with the most stable and warm form of shelter.

1 **Using a shovel, create a large mound of snow.**

It should be at least six feet high. The higher and wider it is, the more room you will have inside.

2 **Allow the mound sit for at least one hour.**

This will allow the snow to recrystallize, forming a sturdier structure.

3 **Build a windbreak.**

While you are waiting, pile snow around the perimeter of the mound, or at minimum on the side facing the wind. It should be several feet high to block the wind from the entrance.

4 **Dig an entrance hole.**

Do this on the side away from the wind.

5 **Carefully hollow out the mound from the inside.**

Leave at least a foot of packed snow for the walls and roof. Use wood or a found object (a piece of metal from a vehicle, old furniture) as a door.

6 **Lay clothing, blankets, or insulation on the floor of the cave.**

Conductive heat loss will occur if any portion of your body is in contact with the ice, including your feet (even in boots). Once inside the snow cave, keep a layer of clothing, a pad or sleeping mat, a jacket, or a bag between your body and the snow or ice surface at all times, and especially while sleeping.

SUPERHEATED

In an overheated climate, a cave will provide the most shelter and climate relief.

1 **Choose a cave with a stable rock type.**

Karst cave systems (those formed by water flowing through limestone, marble, and other dense rock) are usually stable and suitable for long-term habitation. Caves in sandstone, claystone, or gypsum are appropriate as emergency shelter but can be more prone to subsidence and collapse over time.

2 **Avoid mines and mineshafts.**

Disused mines may be inviting but are typically supported with timber that is likely to be very old, rotted, and prone to collapse. Mines may also present fire or asphyxiation danger.

3 **Seek a cave that you can enter at or below sea level.**

The climate in cave systems is directly affected by external weather, including temperature and humidity. A cave in a desert climate may be too hot, while one at high elevation may be too cold for much of the year, even in a warmed world. Ideally, choose a cave system in a milder climate, entered at or near sea level, with limited temperature variability, ranging from a low of about 48 degrees to a high of 52. Even with surface temperatures in excess of 120 degrees, a deep cave should be comfortable.

4 **Choose a cave with an entrance that is large enough to go through but small enough to secure.**

The size of the cave opening often has no relationship to the length of the cave system within: a small opening may lead to a hundred-mile-plus complex.

Caves in the eastern US are often on private land and their entrances may be gated, while those in the West are more likely to be on federal land and unsecured. Choose an open entrance that is small enough to be secured from the inside once your homestead has been established.

5 **Do not inhabit a cave with remnants of bones, fur, or flesh inside.**

The front area of the cave nearest the entrance may be home to bears, mountain lions, and snakes. Use caution upon approach and make your presence known. Bones and bits of fur and flesh indicate the cave is in active use and should be avoided.

6 **After entering the cave, feel, listen, and look for multiple openings.**

A steady and fast wind-flow indicates multiple exposures to the surface and/or an extensive system within. Cave pressure will always attempt to equalize with surface pressure, often causing strong, consistent airflow. If the cave entrance is below other openings, the chimney effect will pull warm air up and out of the cave, chilling it. Caves are usually humid and wind will amplify the cold. Choose a cave system with, ideally, two openings, or, if multiple exposures, small ones that can be blocked.

7 **Assess the cave's stability.**

The presence of large stalactites and stalagmites—formed by the calcification of minerals in water droplets over long periods—indicates that water has been flowing into the cave for many years, making it relatively stable. (Broken formations, however, may be the result of faults or, potentially, other inhabitants.) Piles of rocks and fresh mud indicate regular groundwater or rainwater penetration or sinkholes above, which may make the cave unsuitable.

8 Assess the source of water in the cave before drinking.

Cave water that filters through soil on the surface may contain *Giardia*, a parasite found in feces, and must be purified. If the cave contains a deep lake system fed from below, however, this water is often safe to drink. Even caves in arid locations may contain ancient lakes that are not fed from the surface, though the water may be highly mineralized and not potable. Drink small quantities initially, monitor any intestinal symptoms, and purify if possible (see Dirty Water, page 170).

9 Build a fire.

Caves fill with smoke rapidly and depending on wind-flow it may not dissipate quickly. If possible, build a fire directly under a surface opening where you can take advantage of the chimney effect to draw the smoke out. Shelter in a side passage away from the fire. If this configuration is not available, do your cooking by the entrance, or just outside it. Cook only at night to avoid alerting others to your presence.

10 Check for food.

The cave will likely be home to high-in-protein crickets (see How to Eat Insects and Rodents, page 156, for preparation tips), possibly crayfish and salamanders, and perhaps even so-called cavefish and blindfish—freshwater species adapted to dark environments. Snakes, if present, can also be killed, skinned, and roasted. Bats may come and go and should be avoided.

11 **Barricade the entrance to reduce wind penetration and unwanted visitors.**

Once a suitable cave has been found, use hay bales, tarps, or other material to block the entrance.

12 **Build a shelter in the cave for extra comfort and protection.**

A tent or tarp lean-to within the cave will be easier to keep clean and dry and may provide some protection from the wind.

13 **Look for resources within the cave complex.**

Cave systems may run for tens or hundreds of miles. While it's not necessary to live deep inside a cave, consider mapping the system to locate potential freshwater sources and alternate entrances and exits.

PRO TIPS

▸ Many caves in the western US contain uranium. The presence of silverish, yellow, or green deposits may indicate uranium ore, though its level of radioactivity is likely to be low and not especially dangerous.

▸ Radon is often present in caves, but reasonable air flow should reduce long-term health dangers.

▸ Narrow coal seams, if present, may be a source of fuel for fires.

▸ So-called fissure caves, caused by the vertical movement of granite slabs, can provide reasonable shelter, though they are unlikely to be very deep.

- Sandstone cliff caves on desert mesas may be too shallow and hot in a superheated world, depending on their depth and configuration.

HOW TO SLEEP IN A BEAR CARCASS

1   **Kill the bear.**

Hunting with a high-powered rifle is recommended and has a higher probability of success, and a lower probability of being mauled by a bear.

2   **Size up the carcass.**

For effective shelter an adult requires the body of a full-grown bear, at least six feet tall and preferably taller. A juvenile may be skinned and tanned but its abdomen will be too small to provide adequate space and warmth for an average-sized adult.

3   **Push and roll the bear onto its side.**

You may need to construct a stout lever if the carcass is huge and heavy.

4   **Spread the bear's hind legs and locate its anus.**

5   **Begin cutting.**

Using a sharp hunting knife, puncture the skin above this area. From this incision point, cut through the abdomen all the way to the breastbone. Blood will pool out.

6   **Remove entrails and organs.**

Scoop out and cut away stomach, intestines, lungs, heart, and other organs. Discard well away from you, as these may attract scavengers.

7   **Crawl in.**

Wearing waterproof clothing or wrapped in canvas or a tarp, crawl into the cavity. Pull the sides of the bear around you while curling up into the fetal position. Leave an opening so you can breathe. The remaining mass of the bear will cool over time but should provide reasonable warmth for up to a day, depending on external conditions and the size of the animal.

PRO TIPS

- ▶ Carry an industrial-size trash bag for emergency waterproofing when sleeping in a carcass.

- ▶ Bears have large reserves of fat. If time allows, cut away sections of the fat, place in a container with a wick, and burn for light, like a qulliq, a traditional Inuit seal-blubber lamp.

HOW TO PLANT A SURVIVAL GARDEN

1   **Clear a plot of land for planting.**

Ideally, your garden should have a dedicated fresh water source nearby. The amount of land you need will depend on geography, climate, and number of mouths you must feed. In tropical climates with a year-round growing season and good soil, half an acre might provide vegetables and limited grains and beans for a family of four. Further north, in the middle South of the US (Tennessee, Kentucky) the growing season will be reduced to 200 days due to frost. In the far northern United States, closer to Canada, you may only get 100 to 120 frost-free days. In these areas you may need six or more acres. Even mild drought will severely limit your production unless you have a dedicated fresh water source.

2   **Plant seeds in a Victory Garden fashion.**

Seeds should be planted in single or double rows of crops in bare dirt, with three feet of spacing between rows. Each plant will have space for roots to get nutrients and water, and you can remove weeds easily with a hoe. Seed planting depth will vary by the seed: seed packets should

Plant seeds in a Victory Garden fashion, with high-nutrient crops such as herbs, brightly colored fruits and roots, and greens such as kale, collards, cabbage, and mustard.

tell you how deeply to plant and how close to plant inside a row. If you don't have a seed packet, most crops are happy planted at a depth of roughly two to three times the diameter of the seed. Spacing in the rows varies according to the final size of your vegetable crop. Mark your crops so you remember what was planted where.

3 **Store extra seeds.**

Seeds should be stored in tightly sealed jars, in the refrigerator if one is available, or in a root cellar if not. Moisture and warmth will severely limit seed viability. Place silica gel packets with the seeds to absorb excess moisture. When kept cool and dry, seeds will last many years.

4 **Ensure that 90 percent of your garden consists of caloric crops.**

Caloric crops include squash, pumpkins, corn, and beans. In the US South, use field corn (also called dent corn, due to the dimple on the kernel), which contains soft starch. In colder northern US states, consider flint corn, which contains harder starch and matures faster than dent corn. Dry dent and flint corn kernels can be used for grits, polenta, parched corn, and flour—unlike sweet corn, which is just a short-lived summer vegetable.

5 **Plant the remainder of your garden with high-nutrient crops.**

High-nutrient crops include herbs, brightly colored fruits and roots, and greens such as kale, collards, cabbage, and mustard. Many greens and roots can also be fermented (cabbage to make sauerkraut, pickled beets and cucumbers) to bring out added nutrients and preserve them. Dissolve three tablespoons of non-iodized salt in water to make a brine, then pour it over your vegetables in a jar and press them down beneath the brine. Wait a week to two weeks, then eat or continue to store.

6 **Water and add compost.**

Water only when soil is dry to the touch. Adding a half-inch of compost at the beginning of the season before planting will help plants thrive. Compost all garden waste to maintain humus (organic matter) in the soil. (See How to Build a Composter, page 191, for tips.)

7 **Soak grains and beans before cooking.**

An overnight soak will help remove many of the compounds plants use to protect their seeds. Dry beans, legumes (peas, lentils), and grains can be soaked for up to twenty-four hours to reduce toxins and make them more digestible. (They'll also cook faster, especially the beans.) To quick-soak, boil the beans in salted water and then let them sit off the heat for 60 minutes.

PRO TIPS

▶ Some tubers and roots, including sweet potatoes, cassava, true yams, potatoes, and ginger can be propagated from cuttings or roots. Keep roots or cuttings in buckets of slightly moist leaves and replant them in the spring.

- ▶ If you plant seedlings instead of seeds, they will need lots of sun and should be moved inside when there is risk of frost.

- ▶ Chickens can be fed table scraps and extras from the garden, and their droppings can be used as fertilizer. Consider a small flock, which will also provide eggs (and meat, if you're so inclined).

HOW TO BUILD A COMPOSTER

1 **Gather materials.**

You will need a wood pallet (used is preferable), four five-foot wood posts, a roll of galvanized wire mesh (chicken wire) four feet wide by twenty feet long, a staple gun, pliers, a shovel, a pitchfork or rake, thick work gloves, fertilizer, and soil.

2 **Choose a location with a reasonable amount of sunlight (at least six hours per day).**

This amount of sunlight should allow the composter to remain damp. It should not dry out completely, nor become oversaturated. Select a location with several feet of open space on each side for proper aeration.

3 **Place the pallet on ground.**

The wood pallet is the base of your composter and will allow proper aeration of the pile, as well as prevent the bottom of the material from becoming too wet.

4 **Dig four post holes.**

The post holes should be located at each corner of the pallet and each one should be one foot deep. Place the posts in the holes and refill, packing down the soil so the posts are straight and secure.

5   **Staple one end of the mesh screening to a post, then carefully unroll around the remaining poles.**

Using the staple gun, secure the mesh to each corner pole. Trim off excess with pliers. The mesh will keep deer, dogs, and other animals out, and prevent the pile from spreading too much.

6   **Fill the composter with any available organic material.**

Items that can go in the composter include leaf litter and twigs, peels, rinds, rotten fruits and vegetables, coffee grounds and tea leaves, crushed eggshells, wood ash, and nonrecyclable or soiled paper. Dairy, meat, poultry, and fish (and their bones) can be composted and will add extra nitrogen to the soil. These items may add some odor, and may attract vermin, but are worth composing regardless. If you catch rats, throw them in.

7   **Wait at least two weeks.**

Natural decomposition will be most efficient at 110 to 160 degrees Fahrenheit. The pile should reach this range naturally in about two weeks during late spring and summer. The pile will begin to settle and compact as the natural process takes place.

8   **Turn and water your compost.**

Turn the pile to aerate it about once a month. Add water if the pile is not damp to the touch. (If the pile begins to smell rotten, it's too wet: aerate it more often and/or cover it with a tarp.) If you add new material, turn it once every two weeks. Turning the pile will increase the speed of the decomposition process, and your compost will be ready to use in about three months.

9   **Check color and texture.**

When the compost turns dark brown and crumbly, with an earthen texture, it's almost ready to use. The original material should be broken down and unrecognizable.

10   **When it's ready, remove the compost and allow to sit for two weeks to stabilize and cool.**

You can store it in burlap sacks for ease of transport.

ALTERNATE METHOD

If you are close to neighbors or otherwise in an area where odors or possible vermin may be an issue, dig a three-foot-deep hole and throw everything in it, then cover. With no added aeration from turning, it may take a year for the compost to be ready for use. Try planting melon or pumpkin seeds directly on top of the compost hole. They will be well fertilized and grow nicely.

HOW TO LOCATE OTHER SURVIVORS

1 **Watch the skies for small plumes of smoke.**

Other survivors will build fires for heat and cooking. Because smoke may be a constant presence from disaster-related conflagrations, look (and smell) for small plumes from campfires in areas otherwise not ringed by fire.

2 **Watch the landscape for lights.**

Battery- or propane-powered lights and lanterns are sure signs of human habitation.

3 **Search cities and towns.**

Large (or formerly large) population centers will receive help and resources before sparsely populated rural areas. Survivors are likely to gather in these locations to meet and trade supplies. Keep in mind that cities will be targeted during war or other forms of physical attack, and their roads and bridges and other infrastructure may be damaged or destroyed.

4 **Follow streams and rivers.**

Fresh, flowing water sources will be invaluable to survivors. Check riverbanks for indications of human settlement.

5 **Survey easily defensible positions.**

Mountainsides or hilltops with wide fields of view and limited approaches are good choices for relocation. Survivors may gather in these places, or at least visit them regularly to check surrounding areas.

6 **Visit caves.**

Humans have lived in caves for eons. While natural caves may be hard to spot, disused mines may be repopulated. Use caution when entering or approaching mines or caves, which may be unstable and may contain hostile clans, hungry animals, or both. (See How to Build Shelter in an Extreme Climate, page 177.)

7 **Search the zoo.**

Caged animals will be sacrificed for food in dire circumstances. Where there's meat, there will be survivors.

PRO TIP

Use a small whistle, which is more audible than the human voice over distance, to announce your presence.

HOW TO TELL IF OTHERS ARE OUT FOR THEMSELVES

Look for the following red flags when you meet survivors to determine whether they are truly collaborative or simply out for themselves—and trust your first instincts, which are usually right.

- **They talk mostly about themselves.**

  If they constantly refer to themselves or put themselves first when they speak, they will likely also do this when they act.

- **They repeat back what you said.**

  This could be a sign that they are trying to buy time to make something up, not being thoughtful and honest.

- **They answer your questions but do not ask any of you.**

  This can show a lack of interest in others, and that they may have their own self-interest in mind.

- **They make statements or offers that sound good, but have little detail.**

  Vagueness and lack of details may indicate that they are making promises they cannot keep. Ask for more information, and if they offer something specific, that is good—if not, they may well be making things up to gain an advantage over you.

- **They are not open to feedback.**

  If they react poorly to your input, they are likely to be difficult or dangerous.

- **They fidget and seem nervous.**

  Behaviors such as bouncing their knee, tapping their toe or hands, or touching their hair and face often are a sign that they have something to hide.

- **Their body language indicates that they are untrustworthy.**

  Signs of this include:

  ▸ Looking away rather than looking at you

  ▸ Keeping hands and arms tight or immobile when speaking

  ▸ Voice cracking or going up in tone

  ▸ Throat clearing

  ▸ Redness (blushing) or sweat in face and neck

  ▸ Excessive swallowing and deep breaths before speaking

HOW TO COMMUNICATE OVER DISTANCE

SMOKE SIGNALS

1 Establish a code.

Signaling by smoke is easy and can be useful over distances, but has one great disadvantage: everyone can see it, including hostile clans. Unless you are simply sending your position, create a simple code that only other friendly clans understand. Assign different meanings to different colors of smoke puffs (black, white, and gray).

2 Build a fire pit.

Create a large (two foot deep) fire pit in an open area, unobscured by trees, by digging a depression in the ground. If necessary, line the perimeter with rocks to prevent spread from embers. The pit should not be so wide that it cannot be easily covered with a large blanket.

3 Build starter fire.

Use dry kindling until it is burning well and very hot.

4   **Make the smoke.**

The hotter the fire, the more complete the combustion and the darker the smoke will be. If the smoke is not dark enough, add more wood. If it still appears gray or white, slowly add small amounts of oil, rubber, or plastic. All smoke is toxic but smoke from these materials is especially dangerous and should never be inhaled.

Add grass or hay, damp leaves, or damp wood to a hot fire to lower the heat and create white smoke. Do not completely smother the fire.

5   **Completely soak a thick, heavy wool blanket with water.**

Wring it out so it is damp but not dripping.

6   **Cover and uncover the firepit to create distinct signals.**

Using two people, each person holding two corners, briefly cover the firepit with the blanket, then quickly remove it, then re-cover to create distinct smoke puffs, as necessary.

PRO TIPS

▶   Various chemicals, dyes, and extracts can be used to create colored smoke puffs, though you are unlikely to have these on hand after the apocalypse. In large enough quantities, table salt (sodium chloride) and saltpeter (potassium nitrate) may turn white smoke yellow.

- Smoke can disperse quickly in windy conditions and may be difficult to spot on cloudy days. Hilly or mountainous terrain may also make signaling more difficult as winds can be unpredictable.

- The number three is often used to denote distress or that help is needed in wilderness situations: three signal fires in a triangle formation, three whistles, three smoke puffs, and so on.

SEMAPHORE

Communication via flag semaphore requires both line-of-sight (usually with binoculars or a telescope—otherwise you could just shout) and a sender and receiver well versed in the flag alphabet (see opposite).

1 **Cut triangles for flags.**

You will need two twelve-inch squares of fabric, one red and one yellow. Cut each along the diagonal to form four equal triangles.

2 **Sew a yellow triangle and a red triangle together, as pictured, to form a square.**

The yellow triangle should be at the top. Repeat with the other two pieces.

3 **Fold over one edge of the yellow side and sew to form a slot for a dowel.**

4 **Insert a wooden dowel.**

The dowel should be twenty-four inches long. The six inches sticking out will be the handle to hold the flag.

5 **Sew the flag at the top to hold the dowel in place. It should be snug.**

6 **Stand with your body facing the party you want to signal.**

7 **Send your message.**

Using the semaphore flag alphabet pictured, spell out your message, taking your time to form each letter in turn. Be sure to use the "attention" and "end of word" signals so the other party is not confused. Do not use punctuation. Keep messages short. For example:

E-N-E-M-Y I-S C-L-O-S-E
C-A-N Y-O-U S-E-E T-H-I-S
D-O Y-O-U H-A-V-E A P-H-O-N-E
B-R-I-N-G B-E-E-R

HAM RADIO

1 **Check radio power or connect to battery.**

Very few ham (amateur) radios plug into a wall outlet—and even fewer have built-in batteries. Most will have an external power supply nearby. Look for a marked power switch and turn the radio on. If there is no power, connect the radio to a 12-volt automotive or marine battery that is properly grounded.

2   **Check antenna. Connect one if required.**

Typically, an antenna will already be connected. If one is not present, you will need to build a simple dipole antenna from spare parts.

Run a length of 50-ohm coaxial cable, long enough to get outside and then as high as possible. Secure to a tree or chimney using rope or zip ties. Connect two lengths of insulated wire, each about thirty-four feet long, to the inside ends of the cable and then to the radio antenna.

3   **Turn the radio on.**

4   **Choose the proper band based on time of day.**

Use the buttons labeled BAND to select the 20-meter band (14 MHz). In general, lower frequencies (below about 10 MHz) work best at night, while higher frequencies tend to work best during the day. The 20-meter band (14.0 to 14.35 MHz) is often open 24 hours and is popular among DXers (long-distance radio operators) who attempt to transmit to other continents. This band will have the most traffic. The ability to communicate over a wider area (longer distance) is usually better at night on the lower frequencies, sometimes more than doubling your daytime range. However, these lower bands may be used less often, and are thus less likely to get a response.

5   **Select the proper voice mode.**

Either amplitude modulation (AM) or single sideband (SSB, which has two submodes, upper sideband and lower sideband). In most cases, AM is less efficient and has a lower transmission distance, so focus on SSB.

You will need to select either the upper sideband (USB) or lower sideband (LSB). As a general rule, use LSB for frequencies below 10 MHz and USB for higher frequencies. On the 14 MHz band, choose USB.

6 **Tune in and listen.**

Starting at 14.150 MHz, use the large turning knob to slowly move up toward 14.350 MHz, carefully listening for conversation. While not assured, you will typically hear two or more people having a QSO (ham-shorthand for conversation). The voices may sound oddly distorted, like Donald Duck. This probably means you're slightly off-frequency: make a small frequency adjustment by turning the knob to normalize the voices. You may accidentally be in LSB, so recheck mode.

7 **Transmit and make contact.**

Press the TALK button on the side of the handset and break into the conversation to make contact with the other parties and share information. Release it to listen. Keep in mind that any information you broadcast may be shared with hostile operators, who would like nothing more than to find you and steal your radio (and any other supplies you may have). It is advisable to listen for a period of time to establish both the locations and the intentions of the other radio operators.

8 **Once you have shared the information you wished to share, advise the listeners that you are shutting**

off your radio until a future time to conserve power. Consider telling the other station you will be back on the air every hour, at the top of the hour.

9 In an emergency, make a distress call.

Say "Mayday! Mayday! Mayday!" State your full name, your exact location, the nature of the emergency, and the assistance you need. If the other station can copy you, they will acknowledge your mayday and may try to get additional information.

PRO TIPS

- ▶ Many radios include an antenna tuner which will automatically adjust the antenna to match the band where you're transmitting.

- ▶ High-frequency transceivers that both transmit and receive can produce 1,500 watts and draw over 20 amps, and there is a risk of electrocution. Keep the radio properly grounded.

- ▶ Local AM and FM stations may continue to broadcast civil defense messages during or after an emergency.

- ▶ Never touch the antenna while transmitting or you risk a painful RF (radio frequency) burn.

- ▶ Amateur radio use is strictly governed and requires licensing in virtually all countries, except during true life-and-death emergencies. After the apocalypse, licensing is not likely to be an issue, but before it, unlicensed ham radio use can result in major fines.

Dangerous Creatures and Humans

HOW TO FEND OFF A PACK OF WOLVES

1 **Quickly survey the wolves' postures.**

A tail straight up in the air and ears pricked up are a signal of dominance, and may indicate a wolf is preparing to attack. A wolf may attack from any posture, however.

2 **Do not run.**

Wolves will readily chase prey over solid ground, and are capable of speed bursts up to thirty-five miles per hour over short distances.

3 **Do not crouch down.**

The smaller and more helpless you appear, the more eager the wolves will be to carry out an attack.

4 **Rush one member of the pack.**

Mock-charge one wolf while yelling to scare the rest of the wolf pack away. Wolves are opportunistic hunters, may be timid around humans, and have a strong flight response.

alpha

Mock-charge one wolf in an attempt to scare the rest of the pack away.

5 Throw sticks and rocks at the wolves closest to you to show you are not defenseless.

6 Protect your legs.

Wolves usually attack the lower extremities of their victims to hobble them and then bring them to the ground. Kick or hit the wolves as they approach your legs until you scare them off. If you have a torch, swing it.

7 Move slowly away from the pack.

If on snow or ice, walk slowly toward solid ground. Wolves tend to chase their prey into deep snow or onto frozen lakes in winter, surfaces where hooves of the victim sink or slide. (Wolves' large, padded feet provide a tremendous range-of-movement advantage in these areas.)

PRO TIPS

- Solitary wolves are generally considered more of an attack threat to humans than pack wolves, though a wolf pack can inflict more damage more quickly.

- Wolves may hunt at any hour of day or night.

- The bite pressure of an adult wolf is about 1,500 pounds per square inch. By contrast, the bite pressure of a German shepherd is about 500 pounds per square inch.

- A wolf pack may have thirty members, virtually all of them related.

- You cannot outrun a wolf.

HOW TO FIGHT BIG CATS

1 **Expect an ambush.**

Big cats (lions, tigers, leopards, jaguars, lynx, and cheetahs) are typically solitary stealth hunters and any attack is likely to occur without warning, with the cat leaping from a hidden position. When traveling, pay special attention to areas of tall grass and large boulders or rock formations. The so-called saber-toothed cat species, such as *Smilodon fatalis*, are not true tigers and have different hunting methods (described below).

2 **Using both hands, steer the head away from your head and neck as you kick and struggle to get away.**

A typical attack from the cat's jaws will target the back of the neck, attempting to rip or shear the neck or throat.

3 **Roll onto your stomach to protect your abdomen.**

The animal may swat at your abdomen in an attempt to gut you. Roll onto your stomach for added protection.

4 **Find a weapon.**

Swing a club if you have one, or grab a stout downed tree branch nearby.

5 Strike the cat's head with a hard blow to show you are not defenseless.

6 Do not play dead.

A saber-toothed cat will typically not grab and hold you but instead attempt to inflict a disabling injury and wait nearby for you to expire from blood loss.

7 Climb a tree.

Many cats can climb and leap, but if you can quickly get out of the animal's leaping range (at least six feet), it may lose interest.

8 Run if the cat seems injured or uninterested.

You cannot outrun most large cats, but if the cat is injured or loses interest, run away as fast as you can.

PRO TIPS

▸ Unlike most modern big cats, saber-toothed cats were not solitary hunters but instead hunted in packs, and probably had a social structure similar to that of lions.

▸ *Smilodon fatalis* was a foot shorter than modern lions, but perhaps twice as heavy. Saber-toothed cats were extremely common in what is now the western United States, and thousands of bones have been found in the La Brea Tar Pits in Los Angeles.

HOW TO BEFRIEND A GORILLA

1 **Evaluate the gorilla's behavior.**

A stressed or angry individual is likely to bark (vocalize loudly) and pound, jump on, or slap the ground before attacking. A gorilla that is just tugging at clothes or grabbing at you may simply be curious.

2 **Do not react.**

Do not scream, hit, or otherwise antagonize the gorilla. Even if the gorilla grabs you, it may be playful behavior. Scaring or aggravating the gorilla may provoke it.

3 **Submit.**

Do not look directly into the eyes of the gorilla. Remain quiet. Do not shout or open arms wide to appear larger. The gorilla may interpret these as hostile acts.

4 **Watch for bluff charge.**

A gorilla may make a bluff charge before an attack to frighten potential threats. It may scream or bark, stomp its hands on the ground, and tear at vegetation as it advances toward you. A bluff charge is fast and intimidating and resembles an actual attack.

5 **Crouch down and make yourself as small a target as possible.**

If the gorilla feels threatened during a bluffing display, it may decide to follow through with the attack.

6 **Stay quiet.**

An attack may include severe biting and pounding or tearing with hands. Even if it appears the gorilla means to harm you, do not actively resist or fight back. It will interpret such behavior as threatening and may attack more aggressively.

To make peace with a gorilla, crouch down and make yourself as submissive a target as possible. Do not look it in the eyes.

7 **Groom yourself.**

If the gorilla has gotten hold of you, begin to "groom" yourself—pick bits of dirt or leaves from your skin, clothing, and hair while loudly smacking your lips. Primates are fastidious groomers, and grooming yourself in this fashion may distract the gorilla in a nonthreatening way.

8 **Groom gorilla.**

As the gorilla's grip relaxes, slowly move your grooming hand to the hand that is holding you, showing keen interest in any bits of leaf or dirt stuck in the gorilla's hair.

9 **Remain quiet and continue grooming until the gorilla loses interest.**

PRO TIP

If the gorilla has you in its grip, do not attempt to pry its fingers apart to remove the hand. A full-grown silverback gorilla is incredibly powerful, much stronger than any adult human. Its grip will be vise-like and impossible to open.

HOW TO SPEAK APE

1 **Make clacking sounds with your tongue to announce your presence.**

Chimps and gorillas who have never encountered humans will be more curious than fearful or aggressive.

Nevertheless, it pays not to startle or surprise them. Make a repeated clacking sound with your tongue pressed hard against the roof of your mouth creating suction and then quickly opening your mouth. Consider this your personal signal: the apes will recognize it later and use it to identify your location. Apes do not clack.

2   Listen for calls.

The apes will make excited but soft *hu hu* sounds when they first encounter you. Do not be alarmed. This sound is used to alert other apes to new or unexpected objects and does not denote anger. If you hear a sound like *waa* or *wrah* (called a bark), this may signal that the apes sense danger. Gorillas, which are unlikely to fear humans (or much of anything else), may ignore you completely.

3   Stay put.

Chimps are omnivores and might chase you as they would prey if you run. Instead, sit down at a distance to avoid intimidating them, and allow them to come to you. Gorillas are herbivores and will not view you as a potential meal.

4   Be alert for juvenile displays.

Younger apes will be very curious and approach you right away, and some young males may puff our their chests, make *hu hu* calls, and run around wildly, as if to challenge you. This is all normal teen behavior.

5 **Identify the alpha male.**

The dominant male may be the silverback or gray-haired ape with the largest musculature. However, the top male might instead be more of a "politician," using the big muscle as his number two or "enforcer." He may not approach you immediately but can be spotted by the other apes surrounding him and seeking guidance. Monitor his behavior and calls as you approach the group.

6 **Reach out to greet any apes that approach with the back of your hand.**

All apes use humanlike gestures and hand and foot signals: they grab and shake hands, embrace, bow, and groom. Reach out with the back of your hand as you clack to greet the apes surrounding you. Gently shake a hand or foot if one is offered. Pant softly to send a friendly signal that should not put you at a disadvantage. Apes have a focal point that's closer to their eyes than that of humans, so they may come very close to your face when greeting. This is typical behavior.

7 **Groom the apes.**

Apes use grooming to bond and build relationships. Begin by grooming an ape extremity (arm, leg), and once trust is established, move to a more intimate area like the face and head. Allow the apes to groom you. Continue clacking.

8 **Greet the alpha ape.**

Eventually, you must bond with others in the group to be accepted as an ally. A high-ranking ally like the alpha is especially useful. Consider a food offering to establish trust. Chimps love eating monkeys, especially their intestines. They will be *very* excited to accept this offering of good will: in fact, chaos may ensue. Apes also enjoy honey and fruits like figs.

9 **Bond with the other individual apes.**

Do not be afraid to establish relationships with other adults, including females. Ape societies are political and hierarchical, but the alpha individual may change occasionally, so best to have good relations with all the apes. Be cautious approaching mothers with very young offspring, but do not be afraid of playing with the kids once they are comfortable approaching you.

10 **Demonstrate tool use.**

While apes' tool use is fairly limited, you may get in their good graces by, say, using fire to caramelize fruit, or employing a torch to smoke bees from a hive and grab their honey.

11 **Use gestures to establish trust.**

You can generally get apes to follow you with a "come here" hand gesture, by looking over your shoulder, or by shaking a branch.

Juveniles will be thrilled to be carried on your back. Chimps split into smaller parties and spread out over their territory during the day and will probably walk with you some distance.

12 **Help defend the apes' territory.**

Chimps are highly territorial and often threaten and attack rivals. Once trust is established, the apes may use you to intimidate other ape groups. Do not take part in any physical altercations, but feel free to travel with the group and make your presence known to outsiders.

PRO TIPS

▸ Gorillas are just as smart as chimps and take considerably less time to acclimate to the presence of humans: potentially months, not years. They also tend to be more easygoing and do not usually attack other gorilla groups.

▸ Chimps and gorillas rarely live in the same societies, and do not ride horses. Beware of those that do.

HOW TO ESCAPE CLONED DINOSAURS

1   **Be alert for signs of danger.**

Any dinosaur large enough to attack a human will be audible and/or visible as it moves. Be alert for swaying brush and trees, sounds of breaking undergrowth, or dust clouds created by herds moving across dry terrain.

2   **Listen and watch for bird-like sounds and behaviors—and watch the skies.**

When excited, agitated, or hungry, the beasts may make low-pitched bird sounds, similar to modern ostriches. Pterodactyls and other winged pterosaurs are meat eaters and are also a danger: these creatures have strong beaks but weak legs, and probably will be unable to lift a grown adult off the ground. Pick up babies and toddlers to prevent them from being snatched. Like birds, dinosaurs have excellent visual acuity; their hearing, though not as sensitive as that of mammals, is still pretty good.

3   **Verify group strength.**

Dinosaurs are gregarious and may live in close proximity to one another. However, while T. rex, dromaeosaurs (sharp-clawed raptors), and other predators often travel together, they are not pack hunters, where each member is given a specific role to play during an attack. A group may opportunistically attack a weak or injured adversary, but individuals will not act in concert and are mostly out for themselves.

4   **Assess size of the attacker to decide whether to run or hide.**

A juvenile T. rex has very long lower legs relative to its body size; will be fifteen to twenty feet long; and can run as fast as an ostrich, around forty miles per hour. Adults, by contrast, are bulkier, bigger (up to forty feet long and ten feet high at the hip), and slower, moving at more of a trot. Running at full speed, you may be able to escape an adult pursuing at normal pace. You cannot outrun a juvenile on open ground.

5   **Get to uneven terrain.**

Heavy bipeds like T. rex will avoid uneven footing, since a fall may cause grievous injury. If possible, quickly scramble up a high outcropping of rocks or boulders. Lighter juveniles may pursue you into these areas, though scrambling with very tiny arms is a challenge. Lighter, more nimble individuals may jump some distance.

To escape a T. rex, scramble up uneven terrain with rocks and boulders—heavy bipeds will avoid clumsy terrain. Head toward a cave or crevasse.

6   Quickly move to a cave, crevasse, or other narrow depression within solid rock—the deeper the better.

The opening should be slim enough to prevent the dinosaur from entering or clawing or biting you. Large reptiles are typically not cave dwellers and will have no experience with these areas.

7   **Distract the dinosaur with an easy meal.**

If you have a fresh kill or another potential snack in your shelter, toss it out and away from the cave to distract the dinosaur and, potentially, satiate it. Note that a T. rex is unlikely to become full on a small mammal carcass.

8   **Wait until dark, when the beast may either fall asleep or lose interest.**

Smaller raptors with large eyes may be nocturnal.

9   **If you cannot get inside, prepare for battle.**

Stand with your back to a rocky outcropping to protect your flanks and keep the attackers in your forward field of view.

10   **Light a torch and hold it in your nondominant hand.**

All animals will avoid fire, which is naturally occurring and dangerous. Make quick jabs or swipes at the beast with the burning torch if it gets too close, focusing on the face and, especially, the eyes. With a few exceptions, dinosaurs will be covered with feathers (not hard scales), which will burn. Ideally, the torch should be six feet or longer, so that you can stay out of the dinosaur's reach.

11   **In your dominant hand, hold a long, sharp spear or stick.**

Do not attempt to impale the predator, as you may lose your weapon if it gets stuck.

12 **Make quick jabs or slashes and then pull back, inflicting small wounds.**

While you may be able to penetrate the skin, dinosaurs are thickly muscled: inflicting a lethal wound will be nearly impossible. However, once your attacker realizes you are not defenseless, it may give up.

PRO TIPS

▶ The fossil record shows clearly that T. rex and other apex predators attacked their own kind, at least on occasion. Consider wounding a baby or a smaller juvenile traveling with the herd. Once injured and defenseless, it may become a target for the other dinosaurs, allowing you time to escape.

▶ You can make reasonably protective armor using the carcass of an ankylosaurus, which is fully covered by thick, nearly impenetrable scales. (Think of a giant armadillo but with a huge, spiked tail.) Do not attack, but if you see a freshly killed ankylosaurus, cut away the skin and attached scales from the back. Air dry (or smoke) the skin and scales, then trim to make a breastplate. Be aware that other dinosaurs may be near any fresh kill.

▶ Do not jump into the sea to escape. Plesiosaurs, mosasaurs, or pliosaurs—massive swimming reptiles—may be waiting below the surface.

HOW TO BEFRIEND NEANDERTHALS

1. **Do not surprise them.**

   Neanderthals live in shallow caves or rock outcroppings to protect them from the elements and predators. Do not surprise a Neanderthal by entering a dwelling-cave suddenly or without notice: you may be clubbed.

2. **Do not flaunt your evolved culture.**

   Fancy pelts, impressive jewelry, or motorized tools might make the Neanderthals jealous and prone to kill you for your wares. With Neanderthals, less is more.

3. **Extend your arms and display empty hands to demonstrate you are unarmed.**

   Keep stone tools or weapons hidden, to be used later for trading or defense.

4. **Look for cave wall etchings or drawings.**

   The presence of pictures indicates the Neanderthals understand symbolism and can communicate. Although they will have no formal written language, and perhaps limited abstract thought, you should be able to make yourself understood.

5 **Establish key words and phrases.**

Point to drawings or objects, say their names, and then repeat. For example: "torch," "spear," or "friend." Encourage the Neanderthals to reciprocate using their names for the same objects.

6 **Compliment their pelts.**

Fur and animal skins are highly prized among Neanderthals. Stroke these items and hold them to your cheek while smiling and making noises of satisfaction. Do not attempt this while a Neanderthal is wearing the furs. Extra caution is advised if the furs are worn by a female Neanderthal, as approaching female Neanderthals may be seen as more of a threat by male Neanderthals.

7 **Offer gifts of value.**

Neanderthals can make fire, but their methods are primitive and time-consuming. Offer matches, some candles, or a lighter. An oil lamp would be especially appreciated. They will have tools and weapons made only of stone, wood, and bone. Share any iron or steel items, but be aware these may be used against you, should things go south. Ask for items in return, to establish trust. Point and use a "give" and "receive" motion.

8 **Compliment their food if offered.**

Say "Good bison!" while rubbing your stomach and smiling. If it's undercooked don't complain.

9 **Do not engage in flirting behavior.**

Neanderthals live in small, patriarchal clans of fifteen to twenty individuals. Upon reaching adulthood, males stay with the clan but females move to other clans to find a mate. Avoid flirting with clan members, as they will almost certainly already be paired with a mate who will not take kindly to your advances.

PRO TIP

Avoid arriving with pets. Neanderthals do not domesticate animals and will surely eat a cat.

HOW TO FEND OFF SWARMS

KILLER BEES

1 **Run.**

As soon as the bees swarm or attack you, run. As you run, cover eyes and nose with your shirt to protect this sensitive area, but make sure you can still see where you are running. If small children are present, pick them up and take them with you.

2 **Do not swat.**

Bees are attracted to movement and killed or crushed bees emit a scent that will attract even more bees. Swatting at the bees will make them more aggressive.

3 **Get indoors as fast as you can.**

The bees will follow you indoors, but will become confused by bright lights and windows, and tracking you will become more difficult. Once inside, get under thick blankets and sheets until the bees dissipate.

4 **If no shelter is available, run through bushes or high weeds.**

This will help give you cover and make bee navigation more difficult.

5 **Remove stingers when safe to do so.**

When a bee stings you, it will leave its stinger in your skin. Remove the stinger by raking your fingernail across it in a sideways motion. Do not pinch or pull the stinger out—this may release more venom from the stinger into your body. Do not let stingers remain in the skin, because venom can continue to pump into the body for up to ten minutes. Drag a dull knife or credit card across the skin to help remove stingers.

6 **Do not jump into a swimming pool or other body of water.**

The bees are likely to be waiting for you when you surface.

PRO TIPS

▶ Bees swarm most often in the spring and fall. This is when the entire colony moves to establish a new hive. They may move in large masses—swarms—until they find a suitable spot. Once the colony is built and the bees begin raising their young, they will protect their hive by stinging.

▶ A nonallergic person can survive about ten bee stings per pound of body weight. Painfully.

- Bees can be easily immobilized or killed using liquid dishwashing detergent. Mix detergent with water in a 1:10 solution and spray on bees to immobilize them.

- The Africanized honeybee is a cousin of the run-of-the-mill domesticated honeybee that has lived in the United States for centuries. The *killer bee* moniker was created after magazine reports about several deaths that resulted from Africanized bee stings some years back. Africanized honeybees are considered wild; they are easily angered by animals and people, and likely to become aggressive.

- While any colony of bees will defend its hive, Africanized bees do so with gusto. Regular honeybees will chase you about fifty yards. Africanized honeybees may pursue you three times that distance. These bees can kill, and they present a danger even to those who are not allergic to bee stings. In several isolated instances, people and animals have been stung to death. Most often, death from stings occurs when people are not able to get away from the bees quickly. Animal losses have occurred for the same reason—pets and livestock were tied up or penned when they encountered the bees and could not escape.

LOCUSTS

Locusts are typically solitary desert insects and may not swarm for decades. But when environmental and breeding conditions are just right, they will gather and travel by the billions and devour all food along their way. Desert locust plagues can last several years, lead to famine, and cost hundreds of millions of dollars to bring under control. Take the following steps if a swarm is expected.

1 **Check time of day.**

Locusts do not swarm at night. They become active a few hours after sunrise, then slow down and eventually land and rest at sunset. Swarming activity typically begins in the morning after the sun has warmed the insects, and they may travel one hundred miles per day.

2 **Watch the skies.**

From a distance, the swarm will appear as a dark cloud on the horizon and may be mistaken for a rain cloud.

3 **Check wind direction.**

Locusts virtually always travel with the wind.

4 **Avoid cereal crops and green vegetation.**

Locusts will voraciously consume virtually anything that grows, preferring grasses and cereal crops (wheat, rice, sorghum), followed by fruits and vegetables. They will land on these crops and strip them bare in minutes. Run away from these areas.

5 **Protect your face.**

While locusts do not sting or bite, and tend to avoid humans and animals, they will probably land on you owing to sheer numbers. The biggest danger is of eye injury or suffocation. Protect your eyes and airway as you seek shelter. A swarm may contain 200 million insects persquare mile and can be tens or hundreds of square miles in size.

6 **Find cover.**

Move into a structure or car, if available. Locusts may enter these areas unintentionally but will not seek them out.

7 **Wait them out.**

Once the locusts have desiccated available vegetation, the swarm will move on.

PRO TIPS

- ▶ Locusts are desert insects and are typically found in the old-world deserts of Africa, the Middle East, and India. In 1988, a swarm of locusts flew from West Africa to the Caribbean in 10 days, a trip of more than 3,000 miles. Eventually, humidity and disease killed them off.

- ▶ A swarm of locusts the size of Manhattan will consume as much food in a single day as all the people in New York and California combined.

- ▶ Locusts are an excellent protein source. See How to Eat Insects and Rodents, page 156, for preparation and nutrition information.

Protect your face and get inside a vehicle or building to wait out the swarm. If possible, travel at night when the insects are at rest.

HOW TO FEND OFF HOSTILE CLANS

Adversaries may attempt to attack or infiltrate your clan to steal supplies, take hostages, or occupy an advantageous geographical location. Be ready with countermeasures prepared in advance.

- **Choose a solid defensive position.**

  Ideally, your camp should be elevated and easily defendable. To prevent sneak attacks from other clans, your fort should have a full field of view in all directions (ideally to the horizon but one or two miles at minimum), such as from a mountaintop.

- **Fortify your encampment to slow down the enemy's approach and help your counterattack.**

  Build high, thick walls, deep ditches, wide moats, or a combination of all three to protect your position. Your camp should have no more than two controlled points of access. The hostile clans will likely attempt to burn you out, so be prepared for fires (see below).

- **Maintain a twenty-four-hour watch.**

  An attack is most likely to come under cover of darkness, typically in the hours just before dawn. Sentries should be posted and assigned four-hour shifts to maintain high levels of alertness.

- **Prepare for incendiary attacks.**

  Enemy clans are likely to utilize flaming arrows, trebuchets (long-armed catapults), and other long-distance weapons to set fire to your camp long before they approach gates and walls. Have plenty of water and blankets on hand to control, douse, and smother flames and prevent out-of-control conflagrations. If possible, move noncombatants to hardened shelters or bunkers within the camp walls. Keep your own supplies of oil, gasoline, and propane well protected.

- **Utilize long-range countermeasures.**

  Attack approaching hostiles using rifles and other long guns, if available, as soon as they are within range. Avoid close-range, hand-to-hand combat at all costs. Use longbows or other weapons if guns are not on hand.

- **Pin them down.**

  Attacking clans, like armies, live or die on supply lines. Keep enemies pinned down long enough to expend their ammunition and attack any attempt to resupply. Once their weapons are exhausted, counterattack.

- **Take prisoners.**

  Members of other clans will be valuable as bargaining chips to secure concessions—or your own captured fighters. Treat them well.

Hostile clan leaders, assuming they are strategic, will probably not display insignia or other clear credentials identifying their leadership. Look for those encouraging or commanding others to fight, or wearing fur hats with long horns.

HOW TO IDENTIFY AN INFILTRATOR IN YOUR MIDST

- **Beware of newcomers.**

  Longtime clan members have built trust and established their value to the group. Newcomers should be subject to a probationary period and their access to critical clan information restricted or tightly controlled.

- **Monitor their movements.**

  Pair all newcomers with a trusted clan member who will keep tabs on them. If the new member is spotted drawing maps, surveying weapon or food stores, or casually checking for unlocked doors, these are warning signs.

- **Get them drunk.**

  When inebriated, the suspected spy may reveal red flags such as "Back when I was running with the Backwoods Boys . . ." or "Pillaging is really more art than science."

Beware of newcomers and watch for suspicious behavior, such as taking copious notes and drawing maps.

- **Give the suspect supposedly important clan knowledge and see if it makes its way to hostile clans.**

  For example, let it slip "accidentally" that the moat will be drained for cleaning on Thursday, then observe if you are attacked on Thursday. Do not actually drain the moat for cleaning.

- **Ask questions to establish timeline.**

  Infiltrators will be forced to lie to account for their whereabouts when they were part of another clan. Attempt to catch them in their lie. For example, if they say, "I was a farmer back then," ask, "Which is heavier, a pound of wheat or a pound of sorghum?"

HOW TO MERGE WITH ANOTHER CLAN

- **Determine their biggest needs.**

  Utilizing Maslow's hierarchy of needs, focus your clan pitch using the psychological structure of the human condition. Initially, target the four primary base-level needs: physiological (food and water), followed in order of importance by physical safety (shelter), belonging and love, and self-esteem.

- **Offer empowerment, relationships, and social structure.**

  Humans are social animals and have evolved to thrive in groups. At the same time, individuals want to be enabled and have personal agency. Stress that your clan has a cooperative structure and culture with no status hierarchy, and that all voices are heard (even if you are the decider).

- **Project leadership, strength, and altruism.**

  People are drawn to those who project power, but not self-aggrandizement or tyranny. The most effective leaders hold socialized power. They are motivated to use their power to advance the social good and have a positive impact on the lives of others. While it may be important in the postapocalypse to demonstrate physical strength and courage, stress that these attributes will only be used to improve conditions that meet the needs of *all* clan members.

- **Create an intentional culture with values and goals.**

  Within human groups, some type of group culture inevitably emerges. Clans with clearly defined social norms and established goals will be more successful that those that are reactive or do things on the fly. Carefully explain the values and aspirations of your clan, noting that all decisions are made to further its goals.

- **Make members and prospects feel wanted and valued.**

  Satisfied belonging increases well-being and self-esteem. Bad behavior emerges in groups when members do not feel a sense of belonging and feel threatened or insecure. To encourage and support belonging (and combat dissent), understand the framework of social motives: social worth (others view you as valuable or irreplaceable), a shared model of reality, and a sense of continual empowerment.

- **Provide list of roles.**

  The clan will need gravediggers, intellectuals, and every role in between. Allow prospective members to choose a preferred role that best suits their abilities and interests. To deter the formation of corrosive class hierarchies, mention that roles are fluid, not fixed, and that all clan members will pitch in when and where necessary.

PRO TIPS

▶ Consensus decision making can be time-consuming and is not appropriate for all situations. As clan leader, consider a voting model, or a group discussion arrangement where everyone's opinion is heard and valued. When you need to make the decision for the group, define those times in advance if possible.

▶ To lead effectively, surround yourself with others who hold diverse views and differing opinions. Research shows that even when opposing views are not acted upon, they improve thinking and decision-making.

▶ Clan members should respect your authority, which should flow from your willingness to listen and your emphasis on shared purpose and goals.

HOW TO MAKE A RANDOM CHOICE

Building a new democracy or autocracy is messy. To reduce the chances that fellow citizens will question your authority or decision-making prowess, use one of the following methods to determine outcomes.

- **Coin flip.**

  Use a coin provided by a stranger to combat potential claims of fraud, of fixing, or that the coin is loaded. Show the coin to a second person, the caller, making sure the difference between the sides is unambiguous. (Typically, the heads side will feature someone's head. The tails side will be the opposite.) Using your thumb or with a simple toss, flip the coin into the air and allow a third person to call heads or tails. Do not catch the coin; allow it to fall to the ground. Check for heads or tails, allowing any observers to confirm the result. Should the decision be challenged, flip again, or move to another method.

- **Pick a card.**

  Show two playing cards, one black and one red, to a stranger. Allow the person to examine the cards, making sure there are no secret doubles and that the cards are not marked. Place them facedown on a table. Instruct a third person to flip a card. Check for red or black and proceed with the decision. For example, a red card denotes "clothing is outlawed" while a black card denotes "we're all vegans now."

- **Rock, paper, scissors.**

  Paper covers rock, rock breaks scissors, and scissors cut paper. Ties go again. Best two out of three determines the future of humanity.

- **Draw straws.**

  Make sure one is visibly shorter or marked.

HOW TO WRITE A CONSTITUTION

1   **Choose the desired political system.**

While a representative democracy should be your goal, there are several types of such systems—presidential, parliamentarian, coalitional—each with its own benefits and drawbacks. Parliamentary and coalitional systems tend to factionalize and suffer chronic instability, while presidential governments can concentrate too much power with the executive. If selecting parliamentary, votes of no confidence should only be allowed for major issues, while presidential systems should have strict limitations on veto power. For coalitional governments, consider a strict vote minimum to reduce infighting.

2   **Include term limits.**

Whichever system is chosen, the constitution should enumerate term limits for elected officials, typically no longer than two terms, or eight to ten years total.

3   **Delineate five critical functions.**

Your constitution should, at the bare minimum, enshrine and detail five major points that any effective representational government will require:

- ▶ Leadership transitions
- ▶ Responsiveness to the needs of the governed
- ▶ The ability to deliver services
- ▶ Adaptation to new developments and future changes
- ▶ Fostering an inclusive and diverse community

4 **Delineate critical rights.**

The following inalienable rights should be enshrined in the founding document:

- ▶ No arbitrary search and seizure
- ▶ The right to a trial before an impartial adjudicator
- ▶ Freedom of speech (including political speech), of the press, and of religion
- ▶ The right to run for office
- ▶ Equality before the law

5 **Add parties.**

While political parties may arise organically, they are also key to carrying out the core functions of government, brokering divergent interests, recruiting and vetting potential leaders, and educating the public. If possible, avoid dual-party systems.

6 **Define horizontal accountability.**

The constitution should provide for some type of independent auditor or inspector to ensure that government is held accountable, and to combat corruption and waste.

7 **Include a judiciary and independent electoral commission.**

The founding document should describe the means of creating an independent judicial system to settle future disputes or weigh in on matters of legal interpretation. Term limits should still apply, though they may be longer than for political positions. An electoral commission should run all elections and be free of political interference.

8 **Consider decentralization.**

Smaller units of geographical government and organization (for example: tribes, clans, or villages) are usually more effective in delivering services and easier to scrutinize, and thus easier to hold accountable.

9 **Add an advisory body.**

If remaining survivors are already loosely organized in clans or tribes, consider an advisory panel of tribal chiefs or clan leaders that can make nonbinding recommendations to the government. This will facilitate buy-in and help build compromise.

PRO TIP

Autocracies may be easier to implement initially, but rarely survive transitions of power.

HOW TO ETHICALLY REPOPULATE

1 **Gather volunteers for breeding.**

Assuming there will be some migration and procreation among tribes, you will need 110 nonrelated individuals (with viable sperm and eggs) in your clan for a reasonably diverse gene pool.

2 **Determine food, shelter, and caregiver needs.**

Babies require solid food (eventually), warmth, and care. While a single adult may be able to supervise a handful of infants (at a ratio of perhaps 1:20), as babies grow and become mobile additional supervision will be required (assume 1:8). Similarly, expanding food stores and building adequate shelter will be a priority as the population increases. These jobs should be given to those who are unable or unwilling to procreate. Assume several hundred clan members in total for a sufficient breeding and support force.

3 **Be alert for founder effect.**

Eventually a subset of the initial clan population may attempt to move away and stop interbreeding with original clan members, known as the founder effect. Such outmigration, combined with illness, disease, accidents, and disasters affecting remaining clan members may hinder your repopulation efforts. Be on the lookout for dissent in the ranks, insular groupings within the clan, and rising challenges to your leadership. Expelling rabble-rousers may be necessary for clan cohesion and the repopulation imperative.

4 **Allow natural coupling to take place at the start.**

Humans have been reproducing for tens of thousands of years, and initial pairings should occur on their own, without your intervention.

5 **Offer incentives.**

Over time, long-term, monogamous relationships—as well as those that result in only a single child—may hinder repopulation efforts. Incentivize procreation by offering "baby bonuses" such as additional food, more comfortable accommodations, or access to the "fancy cave."

6 **Join with other clans.**

Combining clans will increase the pool of available mates and offer more genetic diversity, as well as providing additional caregivers. While in no way should you attempt to force procreation (such as via the use of "handmaids"), the larger the group, the more sex that will occur naturally.

7 Adopt.

Orphan children should be brought into the clan and cared for. Eventually, they will be of breeding age, helping repopulation efforts.

8 Regulate but do not outlaw birth control.

Not all copulation needs to (or necessarily should) result in fertilization. Birth control should be available, with the recognition that repopulation efforts must be the clan priority.

PRO TIPS

▸ Agrarian and preindustrial societies rely on human labor to a greater extent than modern, technologically sophisticated ones. The more people you have, the more available labor there will be, assuming necessary food and shelter are present.

▸ If planning repopulation efforts for a base on another planet, do not begin repopulation efforts until the base is established. In addition, cold-stored sperm and eggs may reduce the need for vast initial numbers of virile male colonists, though women of child-bearing age will still be required.

HOW TO REBUILD A UTOPIAN SOCIETY

1   **Establish trust.**

Trust is the glue that holds civil society together. Shared experience among potential community members— and especially the overcoming of adversity—is useful in forming bonds of trust among people and groups. Untrustworthy individuals will sow discord in a utopian community.

2   **Determine guiding principles.**

All members of the utopian society must share the same set of values: without shared goals and principles, the community will quickly factionalize and eventually dissolve. Principles may be situation-specific, but consider the following as a rough guide.

- ▶ Egalitarianism
- ▶ Environmentalism
- ▶ Noncoercion
- ▶ Shared labor and prosperity

- ▶ Diversity (of people, skills, education)
- ▶ Common goals
- ▶ Security and safety

3 **Form an idealistic bond.**

Utopian communities need not be religious. A central animating idea, however, helps cohesion, can guide other values and principles, and will inform a key goal the community works to achieve. Examples include "We believe in worshiping the gifts of nature," or "We believe in Phil, the all-powerful."

4 **Choose an appropriate governing style.**

Government is not the same as leadership. A charismatic, dedicated leader or visionary may help move the community forward even if crucial decisions are made by consensus, committee, majority, or another process.

5 **Clearly define expectations.**

Regardless of how decisions are made, create a codified set of bylaws: rights, responsibilities, rules, policies, procedures, and expectations that everyone is committed to following. Examples include "We expect all citizens of Philastan to love one another, and to willingly jump from the Cliff of Doom at the end of their seventy-fifth trip around the sun."

6 **Maintain a trial membership period.**

Inevitably, some individuals seeking to join your utopian community will not be a good fit. Consider a one-year probationary period for new members to determine if they are suitable.

7 **Understand and appreciate difference.**

Individuals have diverse attributes and experiences to offer and seek different rewards from a utopian community. Some may be naturally driven and highly motivated to physically contribute, while others may be more contemplative or less willing or able to do physical work. Bylaws should be clear on the minimum level of expected work contributions for each member but should leave room for those who offer cultural, artistic, or intellectual support.

8 **Seek to build a spaceship, not a life raft.**

A utopian community will inevitably draw those who are struggling on their own and require safety, security, and food and shelter. Ethical considerations should always play a role in the acceptance of potential members, but each new member must, in some way, help move the community forward into a better future.

PRO TIP

Walden Two by behavioral psychologist B. F. Skinner, from 1948, is a good starting point when considering the design of a utopian community. It suggests organizing members into four loose groups: *managers*, *planners*, *scientists*, and *workers*.

To establish a utopian society, you must first start by building trust and sharing common goals, then establish shared values and agreed-upon roles and responsiblities.

EXPERTS AND SOURCES

Keith Abney is a lecturer in the Philosophy Department and the Ethics + Emerging Sciences Group at California Polytechnic State University, San Luis Obispo. He focuses on ethics surrounding space colonization, robotics, and other new technologies.

Amesh Adalja, MD, is a senior scholar at the Johns Hopkins University Center for Health Security, with a focus on emerging infectious diseases, pandemic preparedness, and biosecurity. He has served on US government panels that created guidelines for the treatment of plague, botulism, and anthrax in mass-casualty settings.

Marcel Altenburg, a captain in the German armed forces for over a decade, served in infantry, specialized infantry, and as commander of a tank unit. He is Programme Leader of Crowd Safety and Risk Analysis at Manchester Metropolitan University in the UK.

Gretchen Benedix, PhD, is a fellow of the Meteoritical Society and Senior Scientist at the Planetary Science Institute in Tucson, Arizona. She studies the evolution of the solar system, asteroids, comets, and craters; Asteroid 6579 was renamed Benedix in 2006 in her honor. She is currently based in Perth, Australia.

Betty Birner, PhD, a linguist, is a professor of linguistics and cognitive science at Northern Illinois University. She has authored numerous books and scholarly articles on semantics, discourse, and linguistic pragmatics.

Sonja Bolger (Migrating Miss) is a full-time travel writer and blogger who has visited 42 countries and 59 UNESCO World Heritage sites. A native New Zealander, she currently lives in Edinburgh, Scotland. www.migratingmiss.com

Bob Bordone, an internationally recognized expert on negotiation, mediation, consensus-building, dialogue, and facilitation, founded and directed the Negotiation and Mediation Clinical Program at Harvard Law School. www.bobbordone.com

Alex Bowman, an aviator with the US Navy for 11 years, served as an F/A-18E/F Super Hornet Instructor-Pilot. He flew combat missions in Afghanistan, served in the Pacific theater, and has more than 370 arrested landings on aircraft carriers. He is currently pursuing a dental degree at the University of North Carolina Chapel Hill.

John Edgar Browning, PhD, professor of liberal arts at the Savannah College of Art and Design, is an internationally recognized expert on vampires, monsters, and the occult. He has contracted, written, cowritten, and coedited 20 books and 100 shorter works on Bram Stoker, *Dracula*, vampires, zombies, horror, monstrosity, and the Gothic. Twitter: @JEdgarBrowning

Keith Cressman, Senior Locust Forecasting Officer with the UN Food and Agriculture Organization, has been providing forecasts and early warning for 34 years to more than 50 countries. He established innovative early warning systems for other transboundary pests, including the fall armyworm and the Red Palm weevil. He lives and works in Rome, Italy.

Allan Crome (director) and **Fabian Maisonneuve** are licensed immigration advisers at New Zealand Shores, specializing in New Zealand Immigration policy and advice, with offices in Hamilton and Nelson. www.newzealandshores.com

Chris Davis, MD, MBA, is an associate professor in the Department of Emergency Medicine at the University of Colorado School of Medicine with expertise in providing medical care in remote and extreme environments.

Judith Donath, PhD, a writer, designer and artist, focuses on the coevolution of technology and society. Author of *The Social Machine: Designs for Living Online*, she is the former director of MIT Media Lab's Sociable Media Group. vivatropolis.com

Vanessa Druskat, PhD, is an associate professor of organizational behavior at the Peter T. Paul College of Business at the University of New Hampshire. Her research focuses on group dynamics, the human need to belong, and team emotional intelligence.

The Earth Impacts Effects Program at Imperial College, London, calculates expected destruction from asteroid impacts. impact.ese.ic.ac.uk/ImpactEarth/index.html

Anna Feigenbaum, PhD, is the author of *Tear Gas: From the Battlefields of World War I to the Streets of Today* and Principal Academic in Digital Storytelling at Bournemouth University in the UK. www.anna feigenbaum.com

Adam Fetterman, PhD, assistant professor in the Department of Psychology at the University of Houston, is director of the Personality, Emotion, and Social Cognition lab, where he has studied Doomsday preppers.

Erica Fischer, PhD, PE, an assistant professor of structural engineering at Oregon State University, focuses on structural systems affected by natural and man-made hazards, including fires and earthquakes. She has conducted post-wildland fire investigations of the 2018 Camp and 2021 Marshall fires.

Joseph Frederickson, PhD, is a vertebrate paleontologist and director of the Weis Earth Science Museum at the University of Wisconsin Oshkosh, Fox Cities Campus.

His research focuses on the paleoecology and ontogeny of vertebrates. uwosh.edu/weis

Josh Galt is the founder of Entovegan, a company dedicated to improving a plant-based diet through the addition of insects and insect-based proteins and powders. www.entovegan.com.

David The Good, survival gardener, is the author of eleven gardening books, including *Compost Everything*, *Grow or Die*, and *Totally Crazy Easy Florida Gardening*, along with two gardening thrillers: *Turned Earth* and *Garden Heat*, starring hero Jack Broccoli. www.thesurvivalgardener.com

Stephen Green is a managing partner at Green and Spiegel, Canada's largest and oldest immigration law practice. A past chair of the Canadian Bar Association, National Section, Citizenship and Immigration, he lives in Toronto. www.gands.com

Larry Hall is the CEO and developer of the Survival Condo series of luxury survival bunkers. A former contractor for numerous defense agencies, he has been building and renovating shelters for more than a decade. www.survivalcondo.com

Catherine Hobaiter is a reader at the University of St Andrews in Scotland, and the principal investigator of the Wild Minds Lab in the School of Psychology and Neuroscience. She studies the evolution of communication and social behavior in wild apes across Africa. Twitter: @nakedprimate

Brenda Holder, a clinical herbalist, is a traditional guide from the Kwarakwante of Jasper and a traditional knowledge keeper of plant medicine of the Cree people. She teaches courses on plant medicine and traditional living skills.

Dave Holder, one of North America's foremost outdoorsmen, spent two decades in the British military and now serves as a wilderness guide, TV survival consultant, college lecturer, and wilderness first aid instructor. He taught survival tactics to the British and Canadian militaries in the Canadian Rockies for many years. www.mahikan.ca

Juan Horillo, PhD, is an associate professor of ocean engineering at the College of Engineering, Texas A&M University, where he develops numerical tools for tsunami calculation and research.

Andrew Karam, a health physicist, is a board-certified radiation safety expert and the author, mostly recently, of *Radiological and Nuclear Terrorism*. He has consulted for the International Atomic Energy Agency and Interpol, among other organizations. www.andrewkaram.com

Christian Koeberl, PhD, is a professor of impact research and planetary geology and the head of the Department of Lithospheric Research at the University of Vienna. He studies impact craters and terrestrial mass extinction horizons. Asteroid 15963, which is 44 km in diameter, bears his name. It won't hit Earth.

Eric Larsen, polar adventurer, expedition guide, and educator, has traveled the most remote and extreme environments in the world, including more North and South Pole expeditions than any other American. He completed a world-record expedition to the South Pole, North Pole, and summit of Mt. Everest within a 365-day period. www.ericlarsenexplore.com

Patrick Lin, PhD, is a professor of philosophy and the director of the Ethics + Emerging Sciences Group at California Polytechnic State University in San Luis Obispo. He writes regularly on AI, robotics, autonomous driving, cybersecurity, bioengineering, and nanotechnology. ethics.calpoly.edu

Vinny Minchillo is a Texas-based car racer, former demolition derby driver, shade tree mechanic, ad guy, typewriter collector, and author of the comedic novel *Spare Me*. www.glasshousestrategy.com

Michael Poland is Scientist-in-Charge, Yellowstone Volcano Observatory, and a geophysicist for the US Geological Survey.

Rolf Quam, PhD, is a paleoanthropologist and professor and chair of the Department of Anthropology and the director of the Evolutionary Studies Program at Binghamton University (SUNY). His research centers on Neanderthal hearing and language abilities.

David Reckhow, PhD, is a professor of civil and environmental engineering at the University of Massachusetts Amherst. He studies drinking water treatment and quality, with a focus on mitigating chemical contamination of water supplies.

Richard Rhinehart, a caver for 50 years, is the author of numerous books, including *Colorado Caves* and *Eighth Wonder: The Story of Glenwood Caverns and the Historic Fairy Caves*. He is a writer and serves as digital editor for the journal *Rocky Mountain Caving*. www.rockymountaincaving.com

Clemens Rumpf, Hugh Lewis, and Peter Atkinson are the authors of "Asteroid Impact Effects and Their Immediate Hazards for Human Populations," an open access research letter in *Geophysical Research Letters* 44, no. 8 (April 28, 2017). www.doi.org/10.1002/2017GL073191

Jean-Marc Salotti is the author of "Minimum Number of Settlers for Survival on Another Planet," an open access article in *Scientific Reports* 10, article number 9700 (2020). www.doi.org/10.1038/s41598-020-66740-0

Anders Sandberg, PhD, is James Martin Research Fellow at the Future of Humanity Institute, University of

Oxford. He studies societal and ethical issues surrounding human enhancement and new technology.

Laurie Santos, PhD, is a cognitive scientist and professor of psychology at Yale, where she teaches, among other courses, *Psychology and The Good Life*, which in 2018 became the most popular course in Yale history. www.drlauriesantos.com

Martin Siegert, FRSE, a glaciologist, is a professor of geosciences and the codirector of the Grantham Institute for Climate Change at Imperial College, London. He uses geophysics to measure the subglacial landscape in Antarctica.

Cameron M. Smith is the author of "Estimation of a Genetically Viable Population for Multigenerational Interstellar Voyaging: Review and Data for Project Hyperion," in *Acta Astronautica* 97 (April–May 2014): 16-29.

Simon Smith, PhD, is a chemist who developed personal protective equipment for industrial, health-care, military, emergency response, and other applications. He retired from an R&D career in 2019.

Agent Smith (a pseudonym) is a former US Marine and current federal law enforcement agent who tracks smugglers and drug traffickers in the United States and internationally.

Wendy Stovall is Deputy Scientist-in-Charge, Yellowstone Volcano Observatory, and a volcanologist in the USGS Volcano Hazards Program.

Richard Sugg, PhD, is the author of *Mummies, Cannibals and Vampires: The History of Corpse Medicine from the Renaissance to the Victorians*, and, most recently, *The Real Vampires*, as well as many other books. He has taught or lectured at several universities in the UK. www.doctorrichardsugg.com

Menno Tas, a Dutch American living on the Kent coast in England with his wife and two children, trained as an economist and has been a CFO for thirty years.

Matt Thomas, managing editor of AmateurRadio.com, specializes in emergency and disaster radio communications systems. www.amateurradio.com

Jonathan Tomkin is associate director and research associate professor in the School of Earth, Society, and Environment at the University of Illinois at Urbana-Champaign.

US Environmental Protection Agency

US Library of Congress

US National Park Service, Division of Fire and Aviation

Scott Wellborn is a member of the Acorn Community, an egalitarian, income-sharing, secular, anarchist, feminist, consensus-based intentional community in Virginia. www.acorncommunity.org

David Wellington is the author of *Monster Island* and *Positive, a Zombie Epic*.

Jennifer Widner, PhD, is a professor of politics and international affairs and director of Innovations for Successful Societies at Princeton University, where her scholarship focuses on the political economy of institutional reform, government accountability, and service delivery.

Mark Yaxley is managing director, Sales, Marketing & Client Services, at Strategic Wealth Preservation, an international precious metals dealer and secure storage provider based in the Cayman Islands. swpcayman.com

ABOUT THE AUTHORS

JOSH PIVEN has been chased by knife-wielding motorcycle bandits (he escaped); been stranded on a chairlift during a howling blizzard (he was rescued); and torn both his rotator cuffs (he had surgery). He lives in a state of paranoia.

DAVID BORGENICHT has been surrounded by alligators, encountered bears, mountain lions, and more, and has lived to tell the tale. He currently lives in Philadelphia, but his go bag is stocked and ready.

Visit **www.worstcasescenario.com** for new scenarios, updates, and more about the world's best-selling survival brand!